Christianity Explained

A tool for evangelism:
Six studies based on Mark

The Narrowgate
Press

Sovereign World
Publishing

Scripture
Union
QUEENSLAND

Enquiries
Christianity Explained
The Narrowgate Press
PO Box 665
London SW20 8RU
Tel: (081) 947 5686
Fax: (081) 944 7091

Sovereign World Ltd
P O Box 777
Tonbridge
Kent TN11 9XT
Tel: (0732) 850598
Fax: (0732) 851077

The Scripture Union of Queensland
800 Kingsford Smith Drive
Eagle Farm
Queensland 4009
Australia
Tel: (07) 868 1344
Fax: (07) 868 1366

ACKNOWLEDGEMENT

No Christian work is completely original, but is a mixture of
creative thought and borrowed ideas, materials and
illustrations. *There is nothing new under the sun* (Eccl. 1:9).

Acknowledgement is made in the following areas: Study
1 is adapted from a talk by a colleague. The book illustration in
Study 2 and the motivational questions used in Study 4 are
used by kind permission of Dr. D. James Kennedy. In the
1960s, the Lay Institute for Evangelism was one of the early
pioneers of the on-the-job training through apprenticeship,
especially in the area of church-based evangelism. Many of the
other illustrations used are of unknown origin.

CONTENTS

The principles behind Christianity Explained...

Preparing yourself for evangelism

1. Spiritual self-preparedness is everything

In John chapter 4, Jesus speaks to the woman at the well. Now there were many good reasons that Jesus could have found for not talking to her:

- He was tired, hot, thirsty and hungry (4:6).
- Socially it was not done for men and women to converse in public (4:7).
- Jews normally had no dealings with Samaritans (4:9).
- Jesus knew that the woman had a bad reputation – he ran the risk of tarnishing his own image (4:17).

Yet Jesus did speak to her. He was spiritually prepared and alert to grasp the opportunity, no matter what the obstacles.

The spiritual preparation of yourself is everything in personal witnessing. As individual believers, we need several types of preparedness:

- Praying for opportunities
- Looking for opportunities
- Equipped to take opportunities

Christianity Explained can help with the third aspect – being equipped to share the gospel. However, the first and second are a matter of personal spiritual discipline. If you are not *praying* and *looking* then by and large the opportunities will pass you by.

2. Capitalising on casual opportunities

Quite often, concerned Christians have good opportunities to speak personally to their friends on spiritual matters. But these opportunities often wither on the vine: they do not lead on to an extended presentation of the gospel.

Note how Jesus capitalises on his passing conversation with the woman:

- The initial discussion over 'physical water' (4:7) provides Jesus with a bridgehead to speak of 'living (spiritual) water' (4:10)
- The woman's aroused interest provides Jesus with a bridgehead to the people of the town of Sychar. 'Come and see…', she says (4:29).
- His ministry to the townspeople provides a bridgehead for an unscheduled stay of two days (4:40). The *casual* conversation becomes an extended *teaching* opportunity.

As stated before, if you are spiritually prepared and aware, quite often you will find yourself in a 'spiritual' conversation.

Christianity Explained provides you with a simple tool for capitalising on that opportunity.

Remember, in personal witnessing *spiritual self-preparedness is everything*.

FOR DISCUSSION

Read John 4: 31–42

1. Verses 31–34   What is the food Jesus says he has to eat in this passage? (Remember the context!)

2. Verses 35–38   Do you consider that there is a ripe harvest in your area? What must be done?

3. Verses 39–42   Why did Jesus stay an unscheduled two extra days with the Samaritans? Does this tie in with the 'proceed slowly' concept?

4. Compare verses 19,29 and 42

How had their assessment of Jesus grown?

Assume nothing

Many traditionally Christian countries, particularly in the Western world, have experienced a significant decline in church attendance this century and particularly since Word War II. This decrease in attendance has led to a corresponding increase among the number of those who would nominally call themselves Christian but have little understanding of the Christian gospel.

This may be illustrated from the situation in England where only 10 per cent of adults and 14 per cent of children are in church on an average Sunday, although 65 per cent would claim to be Christian. Over 60 per cent of the English people have no real knowledge of the Bible or what the gospel really is. The situation is comparable in Wales but not quite so bad in Scotland. Northern Ireland has its own distinctive problems.

When Zeferelli's *Jesus of Nazareth* was shown on television, 35 million people watched it, but there was no obvious increase in church attendance as a result. On the contrary, attendance continues to decline and in many areas of the country there are not enough Christians to have a real influence on society.

The fall is particularly highlighted by the situation in the inner cities and especially London, *which are spiritual wastelands from which Christians have fled and then forgotten.* Dying congregations, closed churches and churches converted into Muslim mosques or Hindu temples are not unusual. The rural areas of Britain also present an enormous challenge. Many villages have not had a resident Christian witness for more than a century.

A Christian minister was talking to a group of students from a large polytechnic when he was interrupted by a female student who said, 'Excuse me, you keep on using a word I don't understand.' He replied 'What word is that?' (wondering if he was using theological jargon again.) She replied in all

seriousness 'God'. This corresponds with something Billy Graham said while being interviewed on BBC Radio in the mid-80s: 'I had not realised how godless Britain had become since my last visit.'

As one writer has commented, 'It is no longer the case of the shepherd leaving the ninety-nine sheep safely in the fold while he looks for the one out on the hills. The ninety-nine are scattered, lost on the hills!'

The author recently took a husband and wife through this course *Christianity Explained.* As they read the New Testament they asked questions like 'Who is Peter?', 'Who is this David?' and 'These Pharisees — are they goodies or baddies?' They are typical of post-war British people, affluent, well educated but almost totally spiritually illiterate.

A world-wide problem

It is our observation that a similar decline has occurred in many other traditionally Christian countries, particularly those in the Western world. There is little understanding of the Christian gospel in any European country and in Australia weekly church attendance in 1955 – 1980 declined from 33 per cent to 18 per cent of the population. Even in the USA there are now clear signs of an increasing nominalism.

What does this mean for evangelism?

In the past, we could often assume that people from traditionally Christian countries had, in their minds, a basic understanding of Jesus Christ and of Bible stories. The job of the evangelist was to build on this platform of knowledge.

This is no longer true in Britain. It is our contention that, in evangelism today, we must begin from the *presupposition that the person you are addressing knows virtually nothing about Jesus, the Bible or the gospel.* In the majority of cases, this presupposition will be correct.

As a result of this diminishing knowledge of God in our culture, 'crusade'-style evangelism has become less and less effective with the passing of time. Not only is it harder to get people to come out to such events, but even those who do make commitments seem to have little idea of what they have done, or why they have taken this step.

Christianity Explained

In this course, the basic assumption is that the person you are taking through it has little or no knowledge of Jesus Christ in any meaningful way. You should assume that he or she has never even opened the New Testament.

This does *not* mean, of course, that you are going to treat the enquirer in a childish or patronising way. It just mean that you should not *assume* any prior knowledge.

In one particular area, this spiritual ignorance is chronic, both inside and outside the Church. This is the area of 'salvation by grace alone' or 'justification by faith'. In a recent group of 11 adults, all regular members of a reasonably vigorous church, all of them said that 'a Christian is a person who tries to live a good life according to the ten commandments', or some associated answer. Between them they had collectively hundreds of years of church attendance and had listened to thousands of sermons and Bible readings!

Yet such an answer is not just a slight deviation from the truth of, say, 5°. It is 180° off course!

A good rule of thumb is to assume that the person you are talking to understands nothing of the gospel until they can tell you, out of their own mouths, what it is.

This course is based on the assumption that the person you are addressing is completely ignorant of Jesus, the Bible and the gospel — even if that person holds a responsible position in your church! In the course of your discussion you may discover that the person knows a bit more than nothing, and you can adjust your presentation accordingly. But you must not assume it.

A wider application

Although this course has been designed for a traditional, yet declining, Christian culture, it is our belief that it also has a wider use.

Because it assumes no prior knowledge of the Christian gospel, it is a useful tool for evangelism in other situations as well — for people who have not been traditionally Christian or where primary first-time evangelism is being undertaken.

We would welcome guidance from evangelists, pastors and missionaries who are working in these situations. Our hope is that *Christianity Explained* could be field tested in a variety of cultures and then constructive suggestions fed back to us. This is already taking place in some countries with good results.

PRINCIPLE 2
Proceed slowly

The dominance of 'quick one-off' evangelism

Since World War II one basic model has often dominated our thinking on the subject of evangelism, particularly in the traditionally Christian counties. We could call this model the 'quick one-off' approach to evangelism, or as one person whimsically calls it, 'one-dump' evangelism.

The quick one-off model comes in various forms, but it usually follows this pattern –

1. A summary presentation of the gospel: A simplified summary of the message of the gospel will be presented to the enquirer(s). This may take the form of an address, as at an evangelistic rally; a memorised précis of the gospel presented to an individual; or the enquirer may be taken through a short tract which highlights the main points of the message.

2. A call to commitment: At the end of a presentation, lasting anywhere from a few minutes to a couple of hours, the enquirer is asked to respond to the gospel in some overt manner, i.e. put up hand, come down to the front, etc. The enquirer is then asked to pray...

3. A prayer of commitment: This prayer expresses a decision to follow Christ. So, quite often after an evangelistic rally, one will hear statements like 'x people prayed the prayer.'

4. An assumption: Because the enquirer has 'prayed the prayer' it is usually assumed that (a) the person has become a Christian, and (b) the person now understands the Christian gospel. So this leads into...

5. A follow-up nurture course: The new convert is encouraged to participate in a nurture programme in which topics such as Bible reading, prayer, assurance, church attendance, witnessing and giving will be taught.

What's wrong with the quick one-off approach?

In many countries the quick one-off approach has served well in the past, and we need to praise God for those who have come to Christ through its use, and those who continue to do so. But it is our contention that this model has become less and less effective with the passing of time. The reason for this appears to have been the growing secularisation of many societies, as outlined in *Assume nothing* (page 9).

In many countries less than five percent of the population have even a Sunday school understanding of the gospel, Jesus or Bible stories.

Even those who have made decisions at evangelistic meetings seem to be ignorant of even basic gospel truths. The assumption made at point (4) above is often erroneous.

During an evangelistic crusade a colleague was able to speak to many of those who had made 'salvation decisions'. He asked them all the well-known question:

> *Suppose you were to die tonight, and God said to you, 'Why should I let you into my heaven?' What would you reply?*

In not one case over 14 nights was the enquirer able to give a reasonable, biblical answer to this question, however simply. In fact, any concept of trusting in the completed work of Christ as the only basis for acceptance with God was totally absent from their understanding. This was not the fault of the evangelist, whose addresses were usually powerful and biblically based. The 'fault' lay in the inability of the hearer to absorb the gospel in one quick presentation. It is not surprising that the fall-off rate from such approaches is so high.

The simple gospel is not simple

Why is it that many people cannot understand even a simplified one-off presentation of the gospel? Let us try to understand the reason.

Recently, a group of Christians were asked:

> *Imagine you were to write a simple, short presentation of the Christian gospel; what biblical or theological concepts would you expect to be in it?*

The answers came back something like this:

1. The character of God (creator, love)
2. Sin
3. God sent Jesus
4. His death for our sins
5. Resurrection
6. Repentance
7. Faith
8. Salvation by grace

The 'simple gospel' will usually contain most or all of these concepts. But remember, many today have virtually no understanding of the Christian message. So, using the quick one-off approach, we are giving a person who knows nothing at least eight brand new theological concepts to hear, understand, digest, and respond to, all in one brief presentation.

It is rather like taking an eight-course meal, heaping it all on to one plate and saying to someone, 'Eat that!' After one or two concepts, people get spiritual indigestion, and begin to make vague statements of assent, like 'Yes, that's right.' But, essentially, they do not understand what is being said.

Learning to teach the gospel

It is our contention that we need to move away from the quick one-off approach as our primary thrust in evangelism. There will be occasions when it will be appropriate, but in general it is becoming increasingly ineffective. We need to learn to *teach* enquirers the gospel and give them time to digest the content.

Christianity Explained seeks to provide one tool for teaching enquirers the gospel

over an extended period of time.

Evangelism in the New Testament

The evangelists in the New Testament appear to have been opportunistic, adapting their methods and, to a limited extent, their message, to each different situation. Consequently, there are examples which approach the quick one-off model, as in the case of the Philippian gaoler (Acts 16:25–34).

However, the evidence in general points to a more extended approach to evangelism. For example:

> *For three Sabbaths Paul reasoned with them from the Scriptures, explaining and proving that the Christ had to rise from the dead. Some of the Jews were persuaded.*
>
> **(Acts 17:2-4)**

So these words seem to explain the general pattern of evangelism in the New Testament: *reasoned, explained, proved, persuaded, argued, contended.* Mostly, the apostles and other evangelists do not seem to have practiced one-dump evangelism, calling for quick decisions. Quite often, it seems that they did not even ask for decisions. Those convicted asked the preacher!

What is *Christianity Explained*?

Christianity Explained is a six-unit presentation of the gospel which aims to fulfil this objective of teaching the fundamentals of the Christian faith. The course is based around the Gospel of Mark, which is chosen for its simplicity. The underlying assumption is that the enquirer knows virtually nothing about Jesus and the Bible.

It is an evangelistic course in that it seeks to lead the person to genuine faith and repentance by the end of the six sessions. It is a low-key approach in that there is no attempt to pressure or manipulate people into a commitment, though the need for a genuine faith-response is clearly and often put.

Each study in the series aims to teach only one point, that is, to hit only one target per lesson. Each unit is also evangelistic in its own right, so that at the end of each unit there is a call to respond to Jesus.

In the first three studies, the course builds

into the hearer's mind some basic knowledge about Jesus Christ and his finished work — that he is the Son of God, his death for our sins, and his physical resurrection. During the first three studies, the enquirer is encouraged to read progressively through Mark's Gospel. (From experience, most adults will do this 'homework'.)

In the remaining three studies we address the question:

> *How does the finished work of Jesus apply to me now?*

Again, each study clarifies only one main teaching target per unit.

A word of balance

It should not be thought that this is to imply that we should give up all evangelistic enterprises which might be called quick one-off. We need a variety of approaches, as St. Paul says, 'that by all means we might win some'. Rather, this is a plea for a general trend or movement in evangelism away from the quick approach to a model in which we learn to teach the gospel.

The two models can actually go well together. For instance, at World Expo '88 in Brisbane, Australia, the two approaches were used in tandem. The 'Pavilion of Promise', a Christian pavilion at the Expo, presented crowds with a quick (45 minute) visual portrayal of the gospel. Those who responded after the presentation were followed up with *Christianity Explained* . In other words, the follow-up was EVANGELISM and not NURTURE.

Several evangelists are using this course as a second phase to their missions. In this way, the quick initial presentation plus the extended follow-up are regarded as a whole. This has proved to be a fruitful combination.

A practical example

Recently a well-known evangelist held a mission at a large suburban church. Instead of the traditional mission services, a creative approach was used:

• The church arranged as many small home meetings as possible. Christians were allowed to come only if they

brought a friend from outside the church. The evangelist spoke at each meeting, giving a condensed gospel presentation.
• At the end of each meeting there was no call for decisions, but people filled in a card similar to that shown on page 34 of this manual. Those who indicated response were invited to do a six-week *Christianity Explained* course. By the end of the mission over 100 non-Christians were doing *Christianity Explained*.

The quick one-off presentation and the teaching model were thus coupled together, and the two constituted the evangelistic enterprise. The follow-up was again EVANGELISM and not NURTURE.

As one involved person commented later, 'It was very effective'.

PRINCIPLE 3
Limited time commitment

Let us suppose you have a friend or relative whom you wish to influence for the gospel. One approach you could take is to invite the person to attend a Bible study group, where perhaps they will hear God's truth being taught. But there are a couple of problems with this approach.

1. The content

The section of the Bible which is being taught in the Bible study group may not be appropriate for a person who is not yet committed to Christ. For instance, your group may be studying the book of Job, which may be ideal for the level of maturity of the believers present. But a newcomer could sit through many studies on the life of Job, still without understanding the gospel. If the enquirer has the tenacity to stay in the group for a year or two he or she will possibly work it out in the long run. But many people will have dropped out before that time is up.

2. The commitment

Most Bible studies go on for months, even years. Now many people are not willing to make that kind of commitment to a 'religious' group, at least not in the initial stage.

When people are invited to do a *Christianity Explained* course, they are told that the course lasts for just six weeks. If they agree to such an invitation, they know they are making a limited time commitment. They know that if they do not enjoy the course, they will only have to endure it for six weeks!

It has been found from experience that a person who is not a convinced Christian is far more likely initially to agree to such a short-term commitment. After the course is finished, it is hoped that he or she will be more willing to continue in a regular nurture group, or similar programme.

You will see that a six-week follow-up

course is built into the programme, which the enquirers are invited to attend. Many times these groups have turned into on-going Bible study and support cells.

In a recent case, six people did the *Christianity Explained* course, and three of them became genuine believers. They are now in an on-going nurture group in which they regularly pray together, read the Bible and share personal details of their spiritual life. But at the beginning, they would have been incapable of doing these things, and would have been frightened off by the very suggestion. The group has since grown to seven members.

The three fears

Imagine that you are not a Christian and a friend asks you to do a *Christianity Explained* course, or to join a Bible study group. What fears do you think you might have about participating in such a group? There are at least three which we need to consider:

Fear no. 1: ANSWERING QUESTIONS

The greatest of all fears is that of being made to appear foolish in front of the rest of the group. People fear that they will be asked questions about the Bible or the Christian faith, and their ignorance will be exposed to ridicule. When they are being invited they need to be assured that this will not happen.

Fear no. 2: PRAYING ALOUD

People are very apprehensive that the group leader will say to them, 'Will you open the session with a prayer?' Again, when inviting people to attend, tell them also that they will not be asked to pray aloud.

In fact, it is strongly recommended that, when you are conducting the *Christianity Explained* lessons, you do not either open or close with prayers. The classes are a fact-finding exercise for non-Christians and, as such, public prayer seems inappropriate. You, of course, should pray for the group members at home, and encourage other Christians to support you in prayer.

Fear no. 3: READING ALOUD

Many people cannot, or do not wish to read the Bible aloud. Assure the person being invited that they will not be asked to do so.

THE INVITATION

When you are inviting a person to do the *Christianity Explained* course with you, assure him or her like this:

You will not be asked to pray or read the Bible aloud, and you will not be asked to answer questions. There will, however, be ample opportunity for discussion.

It is important that this point is made *with* the invitation, not later on.

How to use Christianity Explained...

METHOD 1
Small groups

A number of churches and individuals prefer using a small group approach to *Christianity Explained*. That is, people are invited to join a small group of enquirers to investigate Christianity over a six-week period.

This approach has certain advantages over the one-to-one method, particularly for shy people who may feel more secure in the larger group.

1. Advertising the group

If you are wanting to use a small -group approach, it is suggested that a simple advertising leaflet could be distributed – a sample of such a leaflet may be found on page 25 of this book. This sample leaflet may be copied and used if you so wish. (Fold it so that the word INVITATION appears on the front.)

For such a course, people could be recruited from the following sources:

- Church members may be encouraged to invite or bring along non-Christian friends and relatives.
- Church-goers, whom the minister or pastor feel do not understand the gospel clearly, could be encouraged to join.
- Referrals to the group may be gleaned from people who have done a previous course and have relatives or friends who would profit from *Christianity Explained*.
- The hosts (the Christian couple who provide the home for the series) may invite their friends and relatives.
- Word of mouth.

2. Advertising in the church

If you are going to advertise the group in church verbally, you need to present the idea in the right way. For instance, suppose you stood up in church and announced:

We are running this course for pagan non-Christians and you would be very welcome to come!

You can imagine the sort of response you would get! Nil! A better approach would be:

This course is designed to go over the fundamental building-blocks of the Christian faith. It will not be heavy or deep theology, but it is designed to allow you to check out the simple fundamentals of what Christians believe. You would be welcome to come, or you may know someone who would be interested. Let me assure you that you will not be required to answer questions, to pray or to read the Bible aloud. There will, however, be ample opportunity for discussion.

Such an approach is inoffensive, and has encouraged many to do the six week-course.

3. Group size

It has been suggested that each group be kept as small as possible. The larger the group, the more difficult it is to deal with people's individual needs. With increasing size, there is a law of diminishing returns that sets in!

About five or six enquirers should be the maximum. If the group goes over this number, then it is suggested that it be split.

4. A regular programme

Most churches approach evangelism as a series of stop-start, one-off evangelistic events: a mission; an evangelistic service; a Holiday Bible Club; a coffee morning, and so on. These are good, but...

We wish to encourage churches to set up regular and systematic programmes of evangelism so that outreach is continuous and not spasmodic.

A simple programme can be set up following the school term timetable. The year is divided into three terms of 12 weeks each. A *Christianity Explained* group, or groups can be run in each term.

This would ensure that at least three times a year people have an opportunity to be introduced to the gospel.

5. Christians out of groups

Try to keep known believers out of the group as far as possible, except for those involved. Some well-meaning Christians can't help answering all the questions, while the guests go more and more into their shells.

The only exception to this principle should be when believers wish to bring along an enquiring friend. In such a case, when the enquirer may not be prepared to come alone, an exception should be made in these circumstances, but in no other. You should tell the Christian to take a low profile in the group, and not to say too much!

6. Follow-up

At the end of the course, all members of the group should complete the Course Assessment Sheet (page 59), and be invited to do the follow-up course.

From experience, about one-half to two-thirds of those who have finished the *Christianity Explained* course have expressed a desire to do the follow-up course, including many who have not yet become believers. Some have come to genuine faith in the second course!

METHOD 2
Area visitation

The small group approach may also be tied into a door-to-door area visitation scheme. One such scheme which has been used productively is described below.

1. Programme

- A Christian home is selected in a suburban area and the programme is focused on about 200 homes near the host home.
- A leaflet is then posted through each door of the 200 homes, inviting people to the six-week *Christianity Explained* course. People may be given a variety of choices, such as a daytime women's group, a Friday evening mixed group, a Sunday morning mixed group. (A sample leaflet is provided on page 25. This may be photocopied and used.)
- These 200 homes are then visited to see if there are any people who are interested. On average, six or seven people have come to the groups as a result of the visitation, though this number has varied from area to area. Where there is some interest expressed, the host or study leader revisits these people so that they know someone in the group and will not be coming in as total strangers.

As well as the contacts made in this way, others are recruited from sources mentioned before:

- Church members' friends or relatives
- Church-goers, who may not understand the Gospel
- Referrals from people who have done a previous course
- Friends of the hosts
- Word of mouth

On average, 20 people have been recruited for each course, and then are broken up into a number of groups. Many of those who have attended profess to have become Christians through this course.

2. Follow-up

All who do the *Christianity Explained* course are invited to join the follow-up course. A sample of the suggested material is included in the back cover of this book.

3. Future development

Doing one area of 200 homes per school term a local area of about 5,000 plus homes could be covered once every eight years. However, the basic concept could be expanded to cover two areas simultaneously, which would reduce this time to once every four years, which is a better goal.

4. Personnel

To run one *Christianity Explained* course for one term, the following personnel would be required:

- Course organiser
- Visitation organiser
- Study leader
- Hosts (the home where meetings are held)
- Ideally, a team of ten visitors

One year planner

On the following page is a suggested one-year programme for churches to implement using *Christianity Explained* in small groups.

1. Each term, a number of options could be offered, depending on the size of the church and the number of trained leaders.

2. Each term could be preceded by an invitation or guest service. At the end of each service people would be asked if they wish, to fill in a small card that says something like this:

Christianity Explained

I am interested in exploring Christianity in more detail, and would like to do the six-week course *Christianity Explained.* Please contact me with details.

Name _____

Address _____

_____ Phone _____

---

3. These groups could also be advertised through:

   - Leaflet distributed to church members
   - Members inviting friends and relatives
   - Special services
   - Leafleting the chosen area
   - Home visitation following the leaflet
   - Other advertising (e.g. local papers, etc.)

4. Your church should also set an achievable goal for the year such as: aim to have 20/50/200 enquirers do the course in the next 12 months!

Small groups programme
~ suggested one-year plan ~

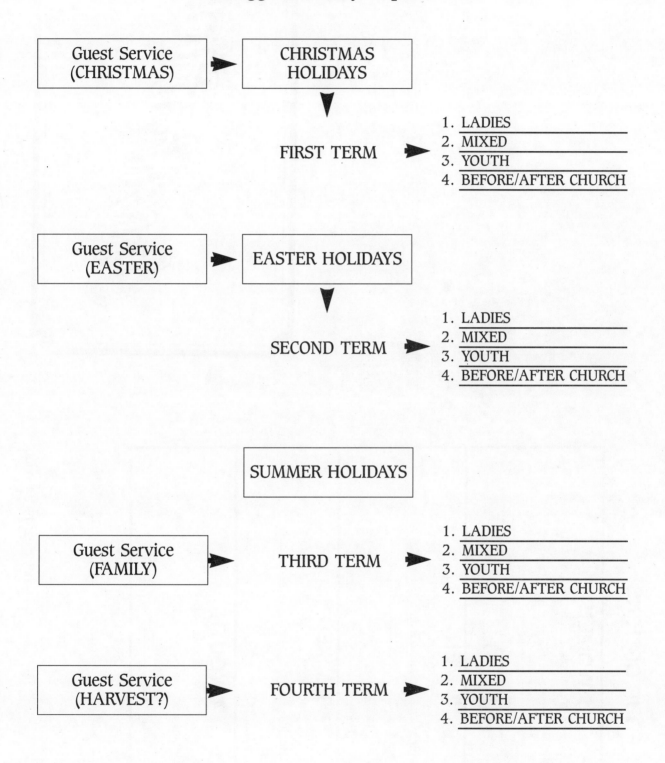

| Guest Service (CHRISTMAS) | → | CHRISTMAS HOLIDAYS |
| | | ↓ |

FIRST TERM →
1. LADIES
2. MIXED
3. YOUTH
4. BEFORE/AFTER CHURCH

| Guest Service (EASTER) | → | EASTER HOLIDAYS |
| | | ↓ |

SECOND TERM →
1. LADIES
2. MIXED
3. YOUTH
4. BEFORE/AFTER CHURCH

SUMMER HOLIDAYS

Guest Service (FAMILY) → THIRD TERM →
1. LADIES
2. MIXED
3. YOUTH
4. BEFORE/AFTER CHURCH

Guest Service (HARVEST?) → FOURTH TERM →
1. LADIES
2. MIXED
3. YOUTH
4. BEFORE/AFTER CHURCH

Invitation

FOUR OPTIONS:

1. WOMEN

Six .... mornings ...... am - ....am

Begins ....

Home of............ ....

Phone..................

2. MEN

Six .... evenings ...... pm - ......pm

Begins ....

Home of............ ....

Phone..................

3. MIXED

Six .... mornings ...... am - ....am

Begins ....

Held at ....

4. YOUTH

Six .... evenings ...... pm - ..... pm

Begins ....

Held at ....

Arranged by ....Church

but open to all.   Child minding can be arranged.

Enquiries ....

You are invited to a series of six talks, plus discussion

Christianity Explained

Is there any hope for the world?
Can I find purpose and happiness?
Where do we go when we die?

• You do not need to know anything about the Bible • You won't be asked to read, pray or answer questions • You will be given every chance to discuss

YOU ONLY NEED AN OPEN MIND!

METHOD 3

Personal witnessing

We have seen in the preceding pages that many people today do not even have a Sunday school knowledge of Jesus, the Bible or the gospel.

Also, we have noticed that the basic approach to witnessing and evangelism in many countries since the 1960s has been on the principle of the quick one-off gospel presentation. But because of the abject spiritual ignorance of so many, the average person simply cannot understand the gospel in so short a time. Even the 'simple gospel' will contain six or seven theological concepts, each of which may be second nature to Christians, but is radically new to the people who are not regular church-goers. Presenting the gospel this way is like asking a person to eat a seven-course dinner heaped on to one plate! He gets spiritual indigestion!

Most Christians today do not have any clear or logical way of presenting their faith to those outside the family of believers. Confronted with a non-believer, the average Christian simply does not know what to say and can only make comments about reading the Bible, coming to church, or talking to the minister, most of which they are unlikely to do.

It is hoped that *Christianity Explained* will provide a helpful tool to the Christian person keen to communicate the faith with neighbours, relatives and friends.

From time to time, most of us find ourselves in a discussion about our faith and the things we believe. Instead of calling for the minister, it is the believer's job to make the most of the opportunity as far as they are able. The enquirer may not want to talk to a stranger or some third party.

It is suggested that in such a situation, *Christianity Explained* may be used to turn a one-off conversation into an opportunity to present the gospel in a digestible way. We have seen previously how Jesus in his discussion with the Samaritan woman began with a casual conversation round the village well:

> '*Give me a drink.*'
> '*How is it you ask me...for a drink?*'

By the end of the incident, however, what began with a chance meeting with one woman turned into a two-day stay, during which time Jesus taught a whole village about the kingdom of God.

Confronted with a similar casual situation you could say to your relative or friend something like this:

I can see that you have got lots of questions about the Christian faith. I know a simple course called Christianity Explained *which just goes over the fundamentals of what Christians believe. Would you be interested in doing it with me? I would be happy to help you in this way.*

Recently a friend who is not a believer came to stay for a week. On the first day of her stay she said to us, 'What have you two got that I haven't got?' meaning, of course, our faith in Christ.

As she was staying for a week, we suggested that each day we might, over supper, sit down and go through one unit of the course. This was a very fruitful time and by the end of the week she understood clearly what we believe. As we suspected, she had many misconceptions of the Christian way! She has not yet become a true believer but is weighing up for herself whether or not to take that step.

At a recent training seminar for the *Christianity Explained* material, a man shared that he was taking a couple of friends through the course. Although the man was in his late fifties and had been a Christian for many years, he revealed that this was the first time in his life that he had ever shared his faith with another person. We later heard that he was training his minister in how to witness!

Many similar examples could be added of people who are effectively using the *Christianity Explained* course as a tool for personal witnessing.

Remember, however, that no tool alone will ever bring a person to Christ. There must be the backing of prayer, and a genuine concern for the state of people around us who are living without Christ. Unless we have the compassionate heart of an evangelist, any tool such as this will just be wasted ink!

Therefore, knowing the fear of the Lord, we persuade men...for the love of Christ controls us.

Paul (2 Cor. 5:11, 14)

METHOD 4

Home visitation by appointment

Behind this method are all three key principles, outlined in the introduction:

■ Key principle no. 1:
ASSUME NOTHING.

■ Key principle no. 2:
PROCEED SLOWLY

■ Key principle no. 3:
LIMITED TIME COMMITMENT

As well as these three key principles, this method is based on two further convictions:

■ Key principle no. 4:
CHURCH-BASED EVANGELISM

Evangelism ought to be done as a general rule by the local congregation.

The New Testament emphasis is on the local congregation as the springboard for evangelism. To the Thessalonians, Paul wrote:

The word of God sounded forth from you in Macedonia and Achaia
1 Thess.1:8

Too often the work of evangelism has been left up to missions or crusade preachers, although these will probably always have their place.

Recently a small experimental programme of *Christianity Explained* was conducted in a suburban church. The known results from this programme well exceeded the effect of a major crusade upon the same suburban area.

■ Key principle no. 5:
CONTINUOUS EVANGELISM

Evangelism ought to be done by the local congregation continuously, in an on-going manner.

Usually, church-based evangelistic efforts are a series of stop-start exercises, such as missions, guest services, children's holiday clubs, etc., which will always have their place, so that, as Paul says, by all means we may win some.

Christianity Explained provides a continuous programme for evangelism. As such it does not have to be large to be effective. The dripping tap will soon fill a basin. Because it is continuous, those involved must be willing to set aside a regular time each week. Irregular involvement makes the programme unmanageable and should be discouraged.

Home visitation by appointment

Most Christians will not do door-to-door visitation on a regular basis. *Christianity Explained* is tied into the normal on-going pastoral visiting by a congregation and is only by appointment – no cold calling!

Three stages of visitation are envisaged.

1. Preliminary or 'fishing' visit

Teams concentrate on visiting people on the fringe of the congregation. A typical approach might be:

Rev. Smith has asked me to help with the visitation of people connected with our church. Could I please drop in and visit you on Tuesday night and bring a friend with me?

During the course of this visit the leader (trainer) seeks to direct the conversation on to spiritual lines. If interest is discerned, the leader describes the *Christianity Explained* course and asks if they can return to do the six studies. They could say something like:

Well, John/Mary, I see that you are interested in this important subject. We run a short course called Christianity Explained *which goes into these things in greater depth. Would you be interested in joining it? We could meet with you, say once a week for six weeks to go through this course, or you could join a larger group doing the same thing.*

You could add that the people in the group will not be asked to read, pray aloud or answer questions. There will, however, be plenty of time for discussion.

If they are responsive, make a date for the first meeting straight away.

If the people being visited are hostile or 'prickly', the leader is under no obligation to suggest the course. Sensitivity must be exercised with no attempt to use pressure against people's wishes.

It may take several such visits to find one person or persons willing to do the course.

The key to this programme is finding enough worthwhile visits to keep the team occupied. Some suggestions for visits:

- Newcomers to church (prime!)
- Regular church-attenders whose commitment is unknown (prime!)
- Fringe adherents of church (prime!)
- Parents of Sunday school children
- Parents of students at scripture/RE classes at school
- Friends of those who have completed the course
- Baptismal enquirers
- Confirmees' parents
- Pastoral contacts
- As a follow-on from other evangelistic thrusts such as guest services, missions, Easter and Christmas services, etc.

2. *Christianity Explained* course
A good proportion of those who have completed this course have expressed the desire to submit to Jesus Christ as Lord and Saviour.

3. Follow-on course (7 weeks)
People will indicate on the Course Assessment Sheet in Study 6 if they wish to do the follow-on course. About two-thirds of those who have completed the *Christianity Explained* course have gone on to do this. A sample copy of an appropriate booklet is included in the back cover of this book.

We now need to consider the question of how to help members of your church to be trained and encouraged to do this outreach work.

Training lay visitors by apprenticeship
Over the years it has been conclusively demonstrated that you cannot train and equip people to be witnesses or evangelists simply by giving them some classroom lectures, no matter how good these lectures may be. You cannot learn to fly a plane or to be a plumber just by going to seminars or by reading many books on the subject. The bulk of the training, to be effective, must take place through on-the-job training.

In developing a programme for regular evangelistic home visitation, you should not be satisfied to do all the work yourself – you will want to train others to assist in this programme. The following is a method which has been tried and proven.

1. Begin in a small way
It is assumed that you may be a person who wishes to pioneer such an outreach programme in the church. You will probably be the pastor/minister or a mature Christian in good standing in the congregation.

First of all, avoid the temptation to initiate a big programme of evangelistic visitation, involving the mobilisation of a large proportion of the congregation. Such programmes tend to lose momentum quickly when problems set in, and there is a high drop-out rate. The writer has been involved in several such programmes which have generally died out in less than two months.

Begin small! Begin by praying that God will give you just one person with whom you could visit, and train in the work of evangelistic visitation. Look for a person who would appear to have latent ability to be trained in this work. Two criteria for such a choice would be a working knowledge of the Christian faith and a reasonably warm and winsome personality. Avoid the temptation to ask for volunteers as you may get people responding out of a sense of duty or loyalty, but who may be unsuitable for this kind or work. Remember evangelism is a gift (Eph. 4:11), and not everyone is equally capable in this area.

Jesus chose twelve disciples by name, he did not ask for volunteers. Can you see him appealing to a crowd, 'Now, who wants to be an apostle?'!

Approach the person you have selected in this way:

Bill/Sally, would you be willing to set aside one evening (or morning) a week to come visiting with me? I want to stress that I will look after the actual presentation of the gospel. You will not be required to do anything except to be friendly and natural. I hope that over a period of time I may be able to train you also to do this kind of work.

The first team then consists of you, the trainer, and the person you have selected, the learner.

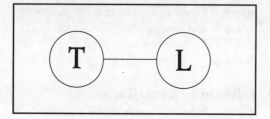

You will notice that by this approach the threat and terror of home-visitation has been removed. The learner is not asked, at least initially, to lead the visit or to present the gospel. He/she is there as an apprentice, that is, an observer experiencing practical on-the-job training.

2. Some classroom training
We want to stress that the learner is engaged in practical, on-the-job visitation from the very first day!

However, there is the need for some 'classroom' training. It is suggested that you meet together for one hour before you go out visiting. So, if you were doing night visitation a suggested timetable might be:

7pm: Visitors meet together for 50 minutes to pray and train
8 pm: Visit in home

A typical timetable for daytime visitation might be:

9 am: Visitors meet together for 50 minutes to pray and train
10 am: Visit in home

This classroom time would have three purposes:

- **TRAINING** To go through the *Christianity Explained* material together. In this situation a learner could practice giving the studies to the trainer.

- **REVIEW** Discussing previous visits.

- **PRAYER** For both current and previous visits.

3. Developing the programme
After sitting through one or two *Christianity Explained* courses, the learner may feel sufficiently confident to visit without the trainer. It is then suggested that two visitation teams could be formed.

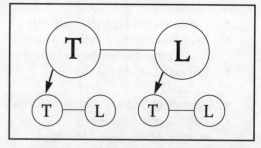

The original learner becomes a trainer and each trainer prayerfully selects another learner to train approaching them in the same way as before.

Thus, over a period of time, a number

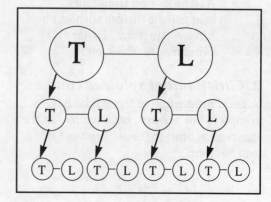

of trained teams could be operating.

In a developed programme, there could be a number of separate programmes functioning:

- **AN EVENING PROGRAMME** visiting those who are not available during the day

- **A DAY PROGRAMME** mainly visiting women

- **A YOUTH PROGRAMME**

Who should visit together? Generally speaking, males should visit with males and females with females. Husband and wife teams, of course, could visit together.

4. NO committees to form!

By adopting this apprenticeship approach, and by beginning small, you will appreciate that you do not have to form any committees, and you do not have to launch into a major campaign to mobilise the church membership as a whole. You can begin with just yourself plus a learner, and a telephone! You can begin straight away!

As the programme grows, of course, some administrative structure will become necessary.

5. Commitment to the programme

By adopting this apprenticeship approach, in general your fellow visitors will tend to stay in the programme, and there will not be the large drop-out rate so typical in an approach based on a seminar or lectures after which those attending are declared to be trained evangelists.

It is strongly suggested that the *Christianity Explained* programme should not be publicised in either the public services or the church bulletin, or prayed for in public. Some of the people you may wish to visit will be sitting in the congregation! However, general prayer for outreach and the work of evangelism may be offered, of course.

What you have heard from me...entrust to faithful men...who will be able to teach others also.
Paul (2 Tim. 2:2)

FOR DISCUSSION

Compare home visitation and the small group approach.

What do you think are the advantages or disadvantages of Method 4 (Home visitation by appointment) as compared with Method 1 (Small groups)?
List them here:

HOME VISITATION	SMALL GROUPS

Some statistics

Having used this course for many years, the author has observed the following average rates of response to the gospel using *Christianity Explained*

1. In small groups

On average, about one person in five who has completed *Christianity Explained* in a small group has made a clear response to Christ at some stage during it. Others have become Christians subsequently.

2. One-to-one

Where an individual has voluntarily agreed to do the course one-to-one, or perhaps a couple, the response rate has averaged about one person in two genuinely turning to Christ. However, it must be said that those who agree to a one-to-one approach are usually more interested and motivated than those who come to a group.

METHOD 5
Evangelistic services

Evangelism in our culture has often centred on the time-honoured tradition of evangelistic services, guest services or missions.

In this model, a well-known speaker is invited to come and preach the gospel, and some form of invitation is given at the end for the people to respond to Christ.

Now let us affirm right away the importance of the prophetic declaration of the word of God. All great spiritual awakenings have contained this element of the heralding of the gospel by people of God full of the Holy Spirit. Although, no doubt, God has used evangelistic services to great benefit in many lives, such enterprises seem to have been decreasing in effectiveness in recent years, especially since the dawning of the age of television.

Any attempt to proclaim the gospel of the kingdom must be commended and encouraged. However, such mission services seem to suffer from the same problems and limitations previously outlined in this course.

For example, we feel that in such services there are three main problems:

1. Too much is assumed

Those present are invited to make a 'decision for Jesus' or a 'salvation decision'. When they do so, it is assumed that they have understood the gospel and are now 'saved'.

Because we make these assumptions, the person responding is then invited to do a follow-up course that covers Christian growth in topics such as prayer, Bible reading, church attendance, witnessing, etc. But there appears to be a fundamental error being made in such reasoning. Let me illustrate.

A Christian colleague was a senior adviser at a recent crusade. When people responded to the evangelist's invitation, they were then spoken to by trained counsellors. The counsellor then took the

person to a senior adviser, whose job it was to ascertain that the respondee had adequately understood the gospel. This adviser asked those who were brought to him the question found in Study 4 of this course: 'Suppose you were to die tonight, and God said to you "Why should I let you into my heaven?", What would you reply?'

In not one case, spread over 15 nights, was the person being counselled able to give any reasonable answer to this question! Not one could simply and clearly outline the gospel! Now the fault for this did not lie with the evangelist, whose addresses were consistently good and powerful. The fault, if we may call it a fault, lay with the inability of the average person to understand the gospel in one presentation.

2. The presentation is too quick

Do not think that this is written against such evangelistic preaching — it is not, but the average person simply cannot absorb the gospel in one quick presentation, however good that presentation may be.

How much better if the evangelist were to say, at the end of the address, something like this:

If you are responding to the message tonight, we want to invite you to join a six-week study group which will look in greater detail at the things I have been saying.

That is, the aim of the follow-up course will not be for Christian growth but for evangelisation. In this six-week follow-up course, the people who have responded will be **taught** the gospel.

The leaders of these groups will then become co-evangelists with the main speaker in the proclamation of the gospel.

Then, after they have understood the basic gospel, the enquirers can go on to look at the growth subjects of prayer,

Bible reading, and so on.

We keep making the fundamental mistake of assuming that when people respond they understand the gospel, and that they are 'saved'. We would contend that neither of these is usually true at this stage. They may become true as the gospel is consolidated in the follow-up phase.

3. The appeal is too narrow

Most evangelistic services are aimed at a narrow group — those who are 'right now' ready to accept Jesus Christ as their Lord and Saviour or to rededicate themselves to him. It is right that our appeal should be addressed to this group.

However there is usually a second and often larger group who may wish to say something like this:

Yes, I am interested in what you said tonight — it strikes a responsive chord with me. However, I am not yet ready to take such a step, although I would be interested in investigating these things further.

Usually, however, we make little provision for this second group. So we wish to offer a practical suggestion which is now being used by some evangelists. At the end of the evangelistic address, each person is given an envelope which contains a pencil and a small questionnaire.

The speaker then asks people to respond voluntarily to the message preached by ticking one or more of those boxes which apply to them. At the end of the service the offertory plates are sent around, perhaps during a hymn, and these questionnaires are collected. The people are assured that they will be dealt with confidentially.

Those who have responded, especially to the first two boxes, are subsequently invited to join a *Christianity Explained* class for six weeks.

In a recent evangelistic service, about 100 people were present and this method was used. Two people ticked the first box indicating that they had received Christ. About 12, however, ticked the second box, asking to join *Christianity Explained.*

Note that it is vital to have your follow-up programme in place before the evangelistic service is held, so that the follow-up takes place efficiently and without delay.

Such a method could also be used for special services such as Christmas and Easter.

The questionnaire card could be worded something like this:

☐ I have decided, for the first time, to surrender my life to Jesus Christ as my Lord and Saviour.
☐ I would like to join a six week discussion group to investigate Christianity further.
☐ I have not yet accepted Jesus Christ, but I would like to receive some literature to help me in this decision.
☐ I have a special need which is affecting my relationship with God and other people. I would like to discuss it confidentially.
☐ None of these are applicable at the moment.

Name _____
Address: _____
_____
Postcode: _____
Phone: _____

Other practical methods

1. BIBLE DISTRIBUTION PROGRAMME

One church has used the *Christianity Explained* course in conjunction with a home Bible distribution campaign. Visitors go from door to door offering people a free copy of a modern translation of the New Testament. When people accept, they are also asked if they would like to do a six-week course called *Christianity Explained*, either in their home, or by coming to a group. A leaflet is given to them explaining the details for the course.

For this type of programme, inexpensive New Testaments are available from the Bible Society or similar organisations.

2. CAMP STUDIES

A number of people have successfully modified this course as camp studies, either for a youth camp, or for an evangelistic adult camp.

3. BAPTISM PREPARATION

In churches where infant baptism is practiced, many ministers are using *Christianity Explained* as a way of preparing the parents for this service. So when the parents ring up requesting the baptism, the minister may respond with something like this:

Thank you for your call. I would be pleased to help you. However, you need to understand that this service is for you, the parents, as well as the child, since you are making promises to bring your child up with respect and love for God. Before I would be willing to proceed with this service I would require/strongly suggest that you do our six-week baptism preparation course.

The *Christianity Explained* course given a baptismal flavour could be used for this preparation. Several ministers have trained teams of lay workers to help them in this work.

4. BELIEVERS' BAPTISM OR CONFIRMATION

Again, several churches are using *Christianity Explained* as the first six weeks of their preparation course either for believers' baptism or for confirmation. It may also be used for wedding preparation.

5. ADULT EDUCATION CLASSES

One person offered *Christianity Explained* as an option through local adult education classes. To her surprise, eight people came, and after the classes wanted to continue as an on-going Bible study group. This, of course, had to be done on a non-denominational basis. See page 81 for some stories from other churches.

6. FRATERNAL CO-OPERATION

In a country town, the Ministers' Fraternal decided to visit half the town and invite folk to a *Christianity Explained* course on a co-operative basis. They prayed for 15 people to turn up, and on the night 75 appeared! The next year they did the other half of the town and another 35 came.

7. CHRISTMAS AND EASTER

Christmas and Easter services are great opportunities for evangelism—what better topics! People often make a special effort to attend these occasions.

They are excellent times to use the questionnaire card and envelope approach as outlined in Method 5: Evangelistic services (see page 33).

The six studies...

Introduction to the six studies

This course proceeds from the assumption that some people in your group will know **nothing** about the Christian faith. Some will not know even the basic Sunday school stories, or where to find the books of the Bible, or the difference between the Old and New Testaments.

We are claiming that we will explain Christianity in only six one-hour sessions. A big claim! Obviously our course structure must be **simple and selective.** We must not try to confuse their minds with a complete course of biblical theology.

The course is split into two halves of three studies each.

- **Studies 1, 2 and 3**
  The life, teachings and claims of Jesus (based on Mark's Gospel).
- **Studies 4, 5 and 6**
  How this applies to me.

---

1. JESUS: SON OF GOD
Homework: Read Mark 1–5

2. JESUS: HIS CRUCIFIXION
Homework: Read Mark 6–10

3. JESUS: HIS RESURRECTION
Homework: Read Mark 11–16

**4. SALVATION:
GRACE NOT WORKS**
Homework: Read tract

**5. SALVATION:
WHAT IS A CHRISTIAN?
(I) REPENTANCE**

**6. SALVATION:
WHAT IS A CHRISTIAN?
(II) FAITH**

Mark's Gospel is used because:

- It is the shortest.
- Its vocabulary is the simplest.
- The opening chapters lack the genealogy of Matthew chapter 1, Luke chapters 1–3, and the difficult 'word' concepts of John chapter 1.

Practical tips for leading a course

1. Opening
Before beginning the first study, it is important to make the enquirers feel relaxed and to overcome their fears and apprehension. As we have already pointed out, people have three main fears:

- That they will be asked to answer questions and their ignorance will embarrass them.
- They will be asked to pray.
- They will be asked to read aloud.

Your opening remarks should be used to remove these fears (see page 15).

2. Christians out of the groups
If you are using the group approach, try to keep known believers out of the group as far as possible except for those involved. As we have mentioned before, some well-meaning Christians can't help answering all the questions while the visitors go more and more into their shells.

3. Seating
Sit in a rough circle. The leader (trainer) should sit in a position in which to be seen easily by all. The learner should look, naturally, at the person who is speaking, which will usually be the trainer.

4. The trainer's role
We are trying to impart knowledge about

Variations to this course

No Christian person has a perfect understanding of God's word, and no gospel presentation will be totally acceptable to every person who uses it.

If you sense a weakness in any part of this gospel presentation, you are free to vary the wording to suit your particular emphasis, provided that such alteration does not seriously change the overall structure and thrust of the course.

- Minor variations are allowable.

- Major structural alterations are not.

In any case, use the course as written the first time through — you may find that your objections on reading are overcome by how it works out in practice! This course has been extensively used and revised, taking into account a lot of experience. Even though at first sight you can't see the logic in the way we suggest you do things, try it first rather than adapt it straight away.

Use of this manual

When you are taking a group through *Christianity Explained* **do not have this manual open in front of you.** Rather, summarise each study on small sheets of paper which can fit in your Bible. Do not try to hide these notes. You are not expected to memorise the course! You are strongly urged, however, to practise each study beforehand.

Jesus – Son of God

The object

The object of this study is to introduce people to Jesus, especially his early ministry. We look at his authority and miracles as pointing to his status as the divine Son of God.

At the beginning

- You will need inexpensive New Testament, (or similar) to hand out where indicated below. Try to use a modern translation such as the Good News Bible.
- Warm introduction to welcome everyone.
- Explain that, although the course is being organised by 'Church X', you are not wanting to push any particular denominational line. Rather, you will be looking at those facts on which there is general agreement among the churches.
- Assure them, 'You won't be asked to pray, or read the Bible out loud or asked to answer questions — there will, however, be ample opportunity for discussion.'
- Encourage them to do the whole six weeks as each study leads on to the next.
- Ask if there are any questions about how the group is to operate.

THE FIRST STUDY

1. Four opening statements

- The title of this course is *Christianity Explained*
- Christianity, as the name implies, is all about Jesus Christ.
- The only records we have of Jesus are the four biographies — Matthew, Mark, Luke and John.
- Over the next few weeks we will be looking at one of these, the Gospel of Mark. (Give out New Testaments and help the group to find Mark.)

2. Study

Begin by looking at Mark 1:1. 'This is the good news about Jesus Christ the Son of God.' What does it mean to say that Jesus is the Son of God? We will see today that it means that Jesus is a person with authority — all the authority of God his Father.

In order, look up these passages making brief comments on each.

(a) MARK 1: 21–28. JESUS' AUTHORITY AS A TEACHER

The people were surprised at the method of Jesus' teaching. He did not quote the thoughts of other Rabbis or teachers. His characteristic way of teaching was, '*I say to you…*'

(b) MARK 2: 1–12 JESUS' AUTHORITY OVER SICKNESS

At just a word this man was instantly healed. The Bible contains over 30 such incidents — the sick, blind, lame, lepers were healed. You might ask the group if they have an experience of spiritual healing — if nothing else the question might be a good 'ice-breaker'.

Mark's Gospel contains many such examples of Jesus' extraordinary authority:

- In a violent storm, he stood up in a boat and commanded the wind and waves to die down, and they obeyed.
- He healed demon-possessed people with a word.
- On three recorded occasions he raised up dead people — even Lazarus who had been dead four days .

(c) MARK 2:1-12. JESUS' AUTHORITY TO FORGIVE SINS

Jesus said to the man: 'Your sins are forgiven.' The religious leaders rightly saw this as a claim to be equal with God. The rest of the New Testament tells us that Jesus is indeed equal with God as God's Son — more than that, he is both God and man in the one person. (Emphasise this point.)

So this is the picture we are building up. Jesus has come into God's creation, God's world, with the full authority of God. There is no part of the creation — animate, inanimate, human or spiritual — over which Jesus does not rule. As God in human form, he also forgives sins. However, there is one more area of Jesus' authority we need to consider.

(d) MARK 1:16-20, JESUS' AUTHORITY OVER PEOPLE

Jesus went to almost complete strangers and commanded them to leave their jobs and families and to follow him.

As the Son of God, Jesus makes the same claim over your life and mine. He calls ordinary people like us to follow him. These four men did. Some whom Jesus called later refused to follow him. In the whole of creation Jesus' authority is never resisted, except by the wills of human beings! God, however, commands us to submit to the authority of His Son. (Emphasise that we are not advocating that they should leave their family or spouse.)

3. Summary

We have seen in this study:
- Great authority as God's Son. He is the supreme master in God's world.
- His claim to be divine
- The need to come to a decision about him. Someone called Jesus the man you can't ignore. You can reject him as a liar, dismiss him as a lunatic or serve him as the Lord.

Introduce the idea of the three-legged stool—the three fundamental concepts which are at the heart of the Christian message.

4. Homework

Ask the group to read Mark chapters 1 to 5. You can photocopy the reading plan onto the back of the handout. They should note any passages which they do not understand or which they would like to discuss. There will be time to discuss their questions and insights at the beginning of next week's study. Distribute handout summary sheet no.1. A clear master for photocopying purposes is supplied later in this book.

FLASH CARD LAYOUT

Lay these out on the carpet or coffee table as the study proceeds.

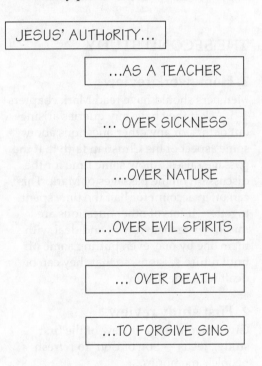

Introduce the idea of the three-legged stool—

Jesus – his crucifixion

The object
The object of this study is to build upon the previous talk, and to show that Jesus did not come only as the greatest healer-teacher. His death and subsequent resurrection are crucial to a basic understanding of the Christian faith.

THE SECOND STUDY

1. Homework review
Members should have read Mark chapters 1–5. Ask if they have any queries arising out of this, or any other questions about some aspect of the Christian faith that the passage raises. Allow some time for the discussion on the passages of Mark. This can often account for half the time spent together. If lots of other questions are raised, write them down, and deal with them one by one, even putting some off until future sessions, so that they can be dealt with adequately.

2. First study review
Give a two-minute review of the first study, 'Jesus — Son of God' to refresh people's memories.

3. The facts of the cross
Read Mark 15:33–38

Explain that the cross is recognised as the central fact of Christianity. The cross has become the symbol of the Christian Church. But what actually happened during the six hours in which Jesus was on the cross?

(a) The darkness (15:33). This supernatural darkness indicated that a supernatural act was taking place. It could not have been an eclipse as it was during the period of full moon at Passover.

(b) The cry (15:34–37). Some people feel that this cry, 'Why have you forsaken me?' expressed some loss of faith by Jesus in His heavenly Father. But we must face the reality of this cry, that at least to some extent God had forsaken Jesus on the cross.

Explain the concept of *substitution* using *The Book* illustration (see page 46). Explain that Jesus took both our *guilt* and our *punishment* (that is, God's wrath) totally in His body on the cross. Add the comment that the resurrection demonstrated God's satisfaction with the work Jesus had completed on the cross.

(c) The curtain (15:38-39). Describe briefly the layout of the Temple, a smaller and a larger room. The smaller symbolised the dwelling place of God, the larger was for the priests as representatives of the people. Explain the concept of *reconciliation* in the tearing of the curtain. The good news is that God and people are restored to friendship.

(d) Ransom (10: 45). Explain the concept of Ransom. This is the payment of a valuable price to buy back a lost person or thing. We can think of examples of ransom payments in the release of soldiers captured in battle, the release of slaves and the redeeming of possessions in a pawn shop (see page 47).

Use the terms 'substitution', 'reconciliation' and 'ransom' only if you feel that they can be understood.

5. Conclusion
Point out that Jesus' death is sufficient for the sins of any person. However, God's forgiveness is not automatically conferred on everyone. If a person does not accept what Jesus has done, he or she is virtually saying to God, 'I don't want anyone to bear my sins — I'll bear them myself.' And so they will, on the last day. We must individually accept by faith the Jesus of the cross.

THE BOOK

A useful illustration of Jesus' death, which can be used in the second study. The object of this illustration is to show visually the meaning of the crucifixion, especially in terms of substitution.

You will need a large thick book, preferably not a Bible. Tell the group that this book represents the life story of any member of the group — from the day of birth (page 1) until the day of his or her death (last page).

In this book is recorded each occasion we have broken any of God's laws — every wrong deed, every wrong word, every evil thought. For example, Jesus says to hate another person is as bad as murder according to God's outlook. To lust after another person is to commit adultery in the heart.

Tell the group that there are many dark pages in your own book which you would not like them to read and, if they are honest, the same will be true for each one of them.

Hold out your left hand, palm uppermost, and say:

Now suppose this hand represents you, and let us say that the ceiling represents God. Now the Bible says that between us and God is what the Bible calls 'the unfavourable record of our debts' (Col.2: 14). *Place the book on the upturned palm of your left hand and keep it there throughout the following explanation.*

So our sins separate us from God. In fact, the Scriptures say that God is so pure that even if only one line was written in this book — that would be enough to separate you from God.

But sin is more than doing, saying or thinking wrong things. It is an attitude of rebellion against God, whereby we ignore Him and run our lives our own way. This is what the Bible means by SIN. This attitude of rebellion is the motive or reason for our many SINS.

Let me make the picture even blacker. The Bible says that, although God is love, he is also a just judge. God hates all evil and *must* punish our sin. One prophet in the Bible describes God in this way: 'Your eyes are too holy to look at evil, and you cannot stand the sight of people doing wrong' (Habakkuk 1:13).

So we have two problems. First, we all have much evil written in our books. Second, God must punish all our evil.

Now, let me try to illustrate what happened during that time when Jesus was hanging on the cross.

Suppose now that this hand represents Jesus. *Hold out right hand palm uppermost, the left hand with the book on it should still be held out.* Again, the ceiling represents God. Now there was no 'book' between Jesus and God. He always perfectly obeyed the will of God. He always pleased His Father.

Now while Jesus was on the cross, God took the sins of people in every age and placed them on Jesus. *Now transfer the book from the left hand on to the upturned palm of the right hand.*

Peter put it this way: 'Christ himself carried our sins in His body to the cross' (1 Peter 2:24) and Paul says, 'Christ was without sin, but for our sake God made Him share our sin...' (2 Cor. 5:21).

You could say that on the cross Jesus became the most sinful man the world has ever seen, as the sins of millions and millions of believers in every age were poured into His body. Then an amazing thing happened. Remember, God must punish all evil. Well, at this moment, God poured upon His own Son on the cross all the wrath and anger and punishment that should fall on you and me. You could say God executed His own Son! Jesus died of the punishment of God. To show that he had completely dealt with our sins and punishment, three days later God brought Him back to life!

Now refer people back to the left hand, now empty, still with the palm uppermost.

Now we must ask how much sin remains between the person who believes in Jesus, and God?

Press the point until someone answers 'none'.

So then, when a person believes in Jesus Christ, God counts him or her as absolutely sinless and perfect in His eyes- in fact, as perfect as Jesus Christ himself.

Go on to stress that this forgiveness is not automatically conferred on everyone, but only on those who accept God's grace by receiving the giver, Jesus Christ.

THE RANSOM

The following can be helpful as illustrations of Jesus' death as a ransom. Like *The Book,* they can also be used in the second study. The idea is that a ransom is the payment of a valuable price to buy back something or someone who has been lost, captured or enslaved.

Use one of these illustrations of the concept of 'ransom':

1. In Roman times, important soldiers who had been captured by the enemy in battle could be ransomed, that is, bought back by paying the price demanded by the enemy.

2. Slaves, in Roman times, could ransom themselves. If they could save enough money, they could purchase their own freedom from their master.

3. Pawn shops have been known in all ages. A person can redeem his pledge by paying the sum demanded by the pawnbroker.

Jesus – his resurrection

The object

The object of this study is to complete this brief survey of the ministry and resurrection of Jesus, and to point out the three facts which a person must believe in order to be a Christian:

- His divine sonship
- His atoning death
- His physical resurrection

THE THIRD STUDY

1. Homework review

Members were asked to read Mark chapters 6–10. Ask if they have any queries arising out of this, or any other questions about some aspect of the Christian faith. Allow some time for this.

2. Review of first and second studies

Give a two-minute review of the first two studies to refresh people's memories.

3. The resurrection: predicted

Begin by pointing out that Jesus on many occasions foretold his own death and rising again. Read Mark 10:32–34.

4. The resurrection: the facts

Read Mark's account of the resurrection — chapter 16:1–8, the briefest of all the gospel accounts. Point out that there are at least ten separate occasions on which Jesus subsequently appeared to His disciples.

5. The resurrection: its central meaning

Ask: as a child, did you ever try to imagine what the world would be like without you? (i.e. If you died?) Comment

that the questions of death and life after death have haunted people in all ages. What happens after death? Is there a heaven, a hell, or nothingness? As one writer expressed it:

> Death itself is nothing,
> But this we fear:
> To be
> We know not what
> We know not where

In the Bible the answers to these questions are found in the resurrection of Jesus. Read Acts 10:39–43.

Point out that Peter has been speaking to Cornelius, a non-Christian. Notice what Peter is saying. These are the things Jesus has commanded to be taught (verse 42). There are five things to note in this story. (Have these points printed on flash cards and produce them one at a time.)

(a) All people will be raised: Verse 42 refers to 'the living and the dead'. The Bible looks to a day when all people living and dead from all ages will be raised. This sounds good, but it may not be.

(b) All people will then be judged: Jesus has been appointed to be 'judge of the living and the dead' (verse 42). We are not free agents. We must all account for ourselves on the day of judgment to the God who gave us life.

(c) The risen Jesus will be the judge on that day: Jesus is 'the one whom God has appointed judge of the living and the dead' (verse 42).

That is why the resurrection of Jesus is so vital. It not only guarantees our resurrection, it also guarantees our judgment. It is to Jesus that we are accountable!

(d) All people will be divided into two groups:

• The positive side:
Those who believe in Jesus – *now*
are forgiven – *now*
are accepted by Jesus – *then*
on Judgement Day (Heaven)

• The negative side:
Read Mark 8:38
Those who reject Jesus – *now*
will be rejected by Jesus – *then*
on Judgement Day (Hell)

Many of Jesus' parables speak of this division. He talked simply about dividing between wheat and weeds, sheep and goats, good and worthless fish.

5. The division is forever.
In the Bible there is no concept of a second chance after death. This life, now, is our one and only opportunity.

Sum up by saying:

Your attitude to Jesus in this life is the same as His attitude to you in the next. If you accept Him now, He will accept you then. If you reject Him now, He will reject you then.
(see also 2 Thess. 1:9-10)

6. Stool illustration
Explain that we have now seen the three fundamental concepts which are at the heart of Christianity.

7. Homework
Ask the group to read Mark chapters 11–16. Members should note any passages which they don't understand or which they would like to discuss. There will be time to discuss these queries at the beginning of next week's study.

Distribute handout summary sheet no.3. A clear master for photocopying purposes is supplied later in this book.

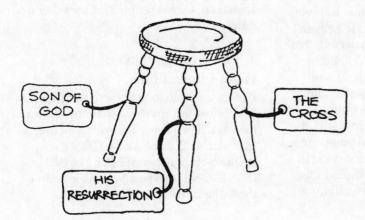

STUDY 4

Grace — not works

The object

The object of this study is to teach the difficult concept (difficult because it is absolutely foreign to proud, sinful human nature), that we are saved by the grace of God in Christ, not by our own efforts or works.

THE FOURTH STUDY

1. Homework review

Members were asked to read Mark chapters 11-16. Ask if they have any queries arising out of this, or any other questions about some aspect of the Christian faith. Allow some time for this.

2. Review of first three studies

A person cannot be a Christian in any biblical sense of that word without accepting three fundamental beliefs.

- Jesus, his sonship (his divine nature)
- Jesus, his cross (his atoning death)
- Jesus, his physical resurrection (his lordship)

3. Introduction to the study

Give out paper and pencils and ask members to write down their answers to two questions. Explain that no one else will see their answers. Begin by asking this question: Do you know for certain that you have eternal life — that is, if you died right now you would go to heaven?

Most people will have answered, 'No' or 'I'm not sure.' Then say, Well, in the next few minutes I'd like to share with you how you can know this for certain. Before I explain this, may I ask you another question that will help clarify the situation? Then ask: 'Suppose you were to die tonight and you stood before God in heaven and he asked, "Why should I let you into my heaven?", What would you reply?'

After they have written down their answers, produce two large envelopes (I suggest 305 x 155mm manila envelopes). (See the diagram on page 52.)

Envelope no.1 has a large X on the back, and the words SALVATION BY WORKS on the front, in bold print. Inside this envelope is another smaller envelope. (I suggest a 235 x 120mm manila envelope). This envelope has the words WHAT I HAVE DONE printed on the front in bold letters, with the word **I** emphasised. Inside this envelope are a number of cards with these words, each on a different card:

My good works; Keeping the Ten Commandments; Not killing; Not lying; Not stealing; Charities; Good citizen; Bringing up family; Bible reading; praying; Church-going; Baptism; Confirmation; Holy Communion.

Envelope no. 2 has a large tick on the back and the words SALVATION BY GRACE on the front, in bold print.

Inside this envelope is a smaller envelope as before, with the words WHAT CHRIST HAS DONE printed on the front in bold letters, with the word **CHRIST** emphasised. Inside this envelope is the completed diagram of the stool we have used in studies 1, 2 and 3. (See diagram on page 52.)

Explain that there are basically only two answers to the question they answered. One is wrong and the other is right.

4. The wrong answer: What I have done

We are going to look at the wrong answer first. Show the envelope with the cross on the back. Then show the words on the front. Explain that SALVATION BY WORKS emphasises WHAT I HAVE DONE. Open this smaller envelope and show the cards inside, one at a time.

Explain that this is how people try to get right with God. But not one of these good works individually, nor all of them collectively, can qualify us for heaven.

Ask the rhetorical question: Why can good works not get us into heaven?

Read Mark 7:20–23

Explain first that God's standard is 100 percent perfection — and by this standard we all fail. This is why no-one can be saved by good works.

Secondly, sin is not just a matter of doing, or saying, or even thinking wrong things. Jesus says here that from within, out of the heart, come all the evil things that he lists.

Suppose you go to the doctor with red spots all over your body, and he diagnoses measles. Imagine he then tried to cure you by putting band-aids over all the spots! You would say, 'Hold on, the spots are only the symptoms — the real disease is within, in the blood-stream!'

So it is with sin. When we do, say or think wrong things these are only the symptoms of sin — the real problem is that from within, out of the heart come these evil symptoms. In our hearts, the Bible says we are in rebellion against God, actively or passively, and doing a few good works cannot cure this rebellion! Doing a few good works is like putting spiritual band-aids on the problem. The central problem is that we each want to run our lives our own way. We want to live apart from God and push Him out. This is sin.

5. The right answer: what Christ has done

Show the tick on the back of the other envelope, then the front with the words SALVATION BY GRACE.

Ask: What do we mean by grace? Explain that this means an undeserved free gift. Take out the smaller envelope to show the words, WHAT **CHRIST** HAS DONE. Open the smaller envelope to show the stool diagram. This shows what Christ has done *on our behalf.*

Read Ephesians 2:8–10.

Explain that it is grace through faith alone that saves us. This salvation is the gift of God. Lay side by side the two smaller envelopes, contrasting WHAT **I** HAVE DONE with WHAT **CHRIST** HAS DONE. Explain that it is the finished work of Christ alone that saves us. We must respond to His finished work by faith.

At this point you may get an objection that could come in a variety of forms, but which will go something like this:

'If salvation is a free gift, doesn't this mean that I can live any kind of life I like — and then so long as I believe, God will forgive me? Does this mean good works are not important?'

Explain from Ephesians 2:10 that God wants us to lead a life of good works, but this is to be the fruit of salvation.

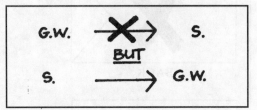

Sketching this diagram may be helpful.

Notice carefully that good works do not produce salvation (Eph. 2:8–9), but salvation produces a life of good works (Eph.2:10).

Look up Mark 10:15 where Jesus emphasises that the kingdom of God must be received like a little child.

6. Conclusion

Recall that you promised to show how they could know for certain that they have eternal life. We have seen that we do not have to earn salvation, indeed we cannot. It is the gift of God.

Finish by saying that any gift must be received. So it is with God's grace.

Next week we will be discussing how to receive the free gift of eternal life.

7. Homework

Give each person a copy of an evangelistic tract — either the one included with this manual or another with which you are familiar. The tract used must contain a prayer of commitment that emphasises the lordship of Christ. Ask members to read it carefully by next week, marking any sections they do not understand or would like to discuss.

Also invite members to read these passages in Mark's Gospel for next week and underline what they think are the most significant words:

Mark 1:15   Mark 8:34-38
Mark 9:43-48   Mark 10:29-31

Distribute handout summary sheet no.4. A clear master for photocopying purposes is supplied later in this book.

THE ENVELOPES
A useful illustration to explain salvation by grace, for use in the fourth study.

THE WRONG ANSWER

THE RIGHT ANSWER

What is a Christian?

1. Repenting

The object
The object of this study is to answer the question: What is a Christian? Begin with a quick overview of studies 1–4.

Homework review
Members were asked to read the little book you gave to them, plus some passages from Mark's Gospel. Ask if they have any questions about the tract, and what key words they underlined as significant in the Bible passages. Why did they see these as significant?

THE FIFTH STUDY

1. Opening
Suppose we decide to go to the shopping centre for a survey. We have only one question: 'In your opinion, what is a Christian?' What kind of answers would we get?

The group members may give such answers as: a good person...goes to church...keeps the Golden Rule...lives in a Christian country...and so on.

Explain that in this session you will deal with this one question: What really is a Christian?

2. Key verse: Mark 1:15
In one sentence, a Christian is someone *who belongs to the kingdom of God.* That is when Jesus becomes the King or Master of your life.

In Mark 1:15 Jesus says there are two things a person must do to belong to the Kingdom of God. What are these?

- REPENT
  (Turn away from your sins)
- BELIEVE

Today we look at Repentance.

3. What is repentance?
You become a Christian when you make Jesus Christ the king or master of your life. In other words:

> I PUT JESUS FIRST...

(Show these words on a flashcard)

Read Mark 8:34–38.

Ask: What does it mean, in practical terms, to repent? It means I put Jesus first in these things:

> ... BEFORE MY WILL

(Add this flashcard.)

Jesus says a person must forget (or deny) self, carry his cross and lose his life. Now the cross was an instrument of death. Jesus tells me that if I am to follow him, I must go through a kind of death experience. I must die to *the right to run my own life* (which is sin). I am to surrender to the God-given right of Jesus to be my king.

Use *The House* illustration on page 55 to help explain what this means.

> ... BEFORE MY AMBITIONS

(Add this flashcard)

Focus on Mark 8:36–37.

People everywhere are trying to gain the whole world. To a small or large degree, their aim is to accumulate power, money, popularity, pleasure, prestige, business success, or just keep ahead of the neighbours.

Now these things may not be wrong in themselves, but they are sin if they are things we live for above everything else. When Jesus is Number One, these things fall into their right perspective. You could quote Jesus' words:

Seek first God's kingdom, then all these things will be yours as well.

(Matt. 6:33)

> ### ...BEFORE MY POPULARITY

(Add this flashcard.)

Focus on Mark 8:38.

It is not popular to follow Jesus sincerely today. Friends or family members may regard me as strange — some may not want to associate with me any more. But if I'm ashamed of Jesus in this life, then he will reject me on Judgment Day! I must follow Jesus openly. He is not interested in secret disciples.

The most obvious way to start doing this is to belong to the church. People who avoid church may claim that it is boring, but often they are just ashamed to be associated openly with Christ and his people.

Emphasise that members of the group may have a spouse, relative or friend who disapproves of their faith. But you must put Jesus first (politely) even if it means ridicule. (Again we are not suggesting a person should leave his/her spouse!)

> ### ...BEFORE MY...???

(Add this flashcard.)

Read Mark 9:43–48.

Jesus does not literally mean that I am to cut off bodily parts. He means that if anything or anyone is stopping me from entering God's kingdom, then radical surgery may be necessary. Point out that pride is often the cause of this.

- Am I too proud to accept salvation as a gift?
- Am I too proud to submit to Jesus as king?

4. Too hard?
Read, lastly, Mark 10:29–31.

It may sound hard to follow Jesus, but he makes two promises when we do:

(1) In this life, he will repay us 'a hundred times' for any cost we suffer.
(2) In the next life, he will give us eternal life.

5. Conclusion
Draw the group's attention to the prayer of commitment in the little booklet. Suggest that they could use this prayer, privately at home, as an act of indicating real and genuine repentance towards God. We will look at this prayer again next week.

You could finish with the summary:

> # Turn
> # Trust
> # Travel

6. Homework
Re-read the tract provided. On the handout sheet, answer the questions from Mark: What gifts does God promise to those who repent and believe?

Mark 1:8
H _ _ _ S _ _ _ _ _ _

Mark 2:10
F _ _ _ _ _ _ _ _ _ _ of S _ _

Mark 10:30
E _ _ _ _ _ _ L _ _ _

Distribute handout summary sheet no. 5. A clear master for photocopying purposes is supplied later in this book.

THE HOUSE

A helpful illustration of the coming of the Holy Spirit into our lives, for use in the fifth study.

To illustrate that when I become a Christian, Jesus comes to live in me spiritually, by his Holy Spirit. Then, over the days and years, the Holy Spirit wants to change me from the inside out, to make me more like Jesus. You will need a plan diagram of a house as shown here.

2. Being a Christian

Point out that the various rooms in the illustration represent all the aspects of my life: MARRIAGE; FAMILY; MONEY; AMBITION; LEISURE; SEXUALITY; TIME; etc.

The Holy Spirit is not content to remain in the lobby. Once he has entered my life, he will want to change me into his image of what I should be like. This does not happen all at once — this is a *progressive* or *gradual* work, like

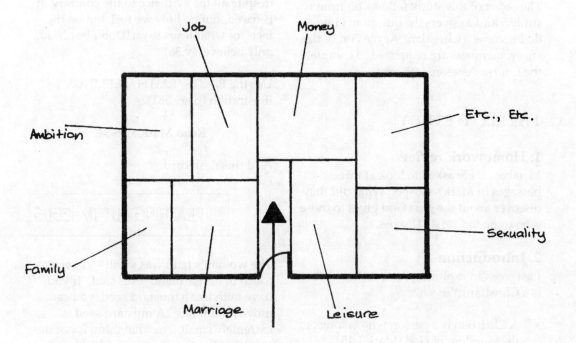

Point out that when you buy a house, there are two stages:

- MOVING-IN DAY
  (This happens only once.)
- RENOVATION AND REDECORATION (This goes on progressively for a long time.)

The same is true of the Christian life: there are two stages.

1. Becoming a Christian

This occurs when God gives me the grace to repent and surrender to Jesus Christ — when he 'opens the door' and by the Holy Spirit comes to live with me. This happens genuinely only once, although many Christians cannot specify the exact day on which it took place. We call this *new birth*, and the believer is *justified*.

renovating a house. We call this *new life* or *progressive sanctification*.

The point is clear. When I become a Christian, I must be willing for Jesus to become Lord of all. This willingness is the beginning of repentance. What this means in practice will be worked out progressively as I grow in this new life, by his Spirit.

STUDY 6

What is a Christian?
2. Believing

The object
The object of this study follows on from study 5 and answers the question: How do I become a Christian? At the end of this study, members are requested to complete the Course Assessment Sheet.

THE SIXTH STUDY

1. Homework review
Members were asked to look at three passages in Mark's Gospel. What did they discover about the gifts God gives to those who come to Christ? Discuss.

2. Introduction
Last week in exploring the question: What is a Christian? We saw:

- A Christian is a person who belongs to the kingdom of God (Mark 1:15), that is has Jesus Christ as king.
- To belong to this kingdom I must REPENT (last time).
- To belong to this Kingdom I must BELIEVE (today's study).

3. What is faith, or believing?
Explain that we are going to look at three incidents from Mark's Gospel which illustrate faith.

Read Mark 5:21-24, 5:35-43.

Display these flash cards:

> FAITH IS...

> ...TAKING JESUS AT HIS WORD

How would Jairus have felt when the message came that his daughter was dead? Faith here is trust in Jesus' words, despite all the evidence to the contrary. It is based, not on how we feel, but on the facts of what Jesus says: 'Don't be afraid, only believe' (v.36)

Use the FACTS/FAITH/FEELINGS illustration (page 58).

Read Mark 5:25-34.

Add this flash card:

> ... REACHING OUT TO JESUS

The woman's faith was small — a secret touch of his garment. Jesus said, 'If you have faith like a mustard seed, you can move mountains.' A mustard seed is extremely small. The vital thing is not the quantity, but the direction of faith!
  Jesus does not allow the woman to remain hidden in the crowd. She was required to show herself publicly. If I am to follow him, I must do so openly, and not be ashamed of him.

Read Mark 10:13–16.

Add this flash card:

> ...HAVING CHILD-LIKE TRUST

Note that this is not child-like faith that Jesus speaks about. This is more than giving mere assent with my mind. It means trust such as a child places in its parents. Use the BLONDIN illustration here (page 58).

Read John 5:24.

Add this flash card:

> ...KNOWING GOD ACCEPTS ME

This tells the believer something about the present and something about the future.

(a) Present: 'he...has eternal life'. Point out the present tense, has. It is not boasting to say, 'I know I have eternal life.' It is just taking God at his word, i.e. it is faith. Nor is it saying, 'I am good.' It is saying that what Jesus has done, not what I have done, makes me acceptable to God.

(b) Future: 'he will not be judged'. Jesus is talking here about the judgment which determines our eternal future, heaven or hell. The believer will not face that judgement, as no charge can be brought against him/her.

Add this flash card:

> ...RECEIVING JESUS
> AS YOUR KING

Recall Jesus' words:

Whoever does not receive the kingdom of God like a child will never enter it.
(Mark 10:15)

We have seen that, to receive the kingdom of God, a person must receive Jesus Christ as their Lord or King, and their saviour from sin. This is a personal step. No one can take it for you.

4. Conclusion

At this point you can conclude the course in one of two ways: You can take the low-key option or the more-direct option.

Many Christians have great difficulty actually leading a person to a commitment to Christ. If this is true of you, the leader, then use the low-key option — this is quite legitimate, and is not being cowardly or anything like that.

A low-key option

• Say something like this: During this course, God may have been speaking to you spiritually. You may feel ready to take the step of receiving Jesus Christ as your Lord and Saviour. I would like to help you to take this step.

• Ask them to turn to the prayer of commitment in *Journey into Life* or the tract you have used.

• Read the prayer to them.

• Suggest that, in the quietness of their own home, they could pray this prayer as a way of saying 'yes' to God.

• Ask them to tell you if they do take this step, so that you can help in the future.

A more direct option

If you are certain in your mind that they are ready to take this step of commitment, conclude like this:

• During this course God may have been speaking to you spiritually and you may feel that you are ready to take the step of receiving Jesus Christ as your king and saviour.

• Ask them to turn to the prayer of commitment in *Journey into Life* or the tract you have used.

• Read the prayer aloud. Then add this comment: I am going to pray this prayer again slowly. If you wish to take this step, I invite you to pray this prayer with me.

• Pray the prayer again aloud, slowly, together.

A word of caution

The Holy Spirit is sovereign in evangelism. Only he can truly convert the heart and mind of a person.

It brings no honour to God if we trick or manipulate people into making decisions they are not ready to make, merely to gratify our own egos.

If you are in any doubt as to whether any person in the group is ready to take this step of commitment, then use the low-key option.

5. Course assessment

Give each person a copy of the Course Assessment Sheet and a pen (see page 59).

Point out that there is no obligation to answer any or all of the questions.

Collect the sheets at the end.

6. Follow-on course on discipleship

Draw particular attention to Question 6 when you are going through the Course Assessment Sheet. If they have agreed to join the course, make arrangements to begin this with them.

FACTS, FAITH AND FEELINGS

A helpful illustration on faith to be used in the sixth study.

The object of this old illustration is to demonstrate that Christian faith does not

Three men are walking along the top of a narrow wall. The first man is called Facts, the second Faith and the last, Feelings.

As long as the middle man, Faith, keeps his eyes on Facts, he can walk securely and steadily on the wall. If he turns around and looks over his shoulder

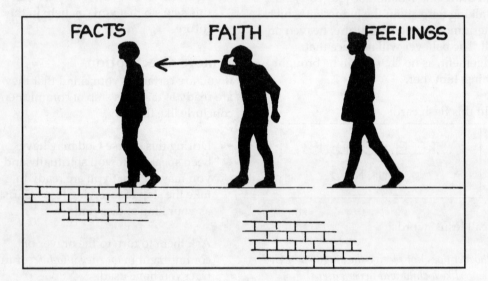

depend upon our feelings, which are always changing, but upon the facts of what God has done through Jesus as recorded in the Bible. These facts never change.

You can use this illustration verbally, but a drawing like this may be helpful.

at Feelings, he starts to wobble and feel insecure.

Similarly, in the Christian faith, solid faith is based on the facts of Jesus as learned in the Bible. If we go too much by feelings, our faith will always be unsteady and weak.

A STORY OF BLONDIN

A helpful illustration to explain faith, for use in the sixth study.

The purpose is to show that it is possible to believe the gospel academically and theoretically without being committed to Jesus Christ personally.

Blondin was a famous trick-stunt high-wire artist in America. Some years ago he stretched a wire rope across the top of Niagara Falls and walked across it.

Next he announced that he was going to wheel a man in a wheelbarrow across

the wire.

A newspaper reporter came to interview Blondin about this proposed stunt: 'Do you think I can do this great feat?' Blondin asked the reporter.

'I really believe you can,' replied the reporter. 'I think you are the greatest stunt artist of all time!'

'You believe I can do it?' asked Blondin, 'Well then, you get in the wheelbarrow!'

There is a great difference between believing something or in someone theoretically and being willing to commit your life into his or her hands by faith.

Christianity Explained course assessment

Tick appropriate answers.
Please be honest and frank.
Please feel free not to answer any of these questions.

Name .... Phone...................................

1. **Before you began this course, how would you have described yourself?**
    a. ☐ I didn't believe in God.
    b. ☐ I didn't know if there was a God or not.
    c   ☐ I believed in God, but not in Jesus Christ.
    d. ☐ I thought I was a Christian, but now I know I was not.
    e. ☐ A Christian (ie. a personal commitment to Jesus Christ).
    f. ☐ Something else ....

2. **How would you assess your position now in relation to Jesus Christ?**
    a. ☐ I have genuinely repented and come to believe in Jesus, and I have received him as my lord and
        saviour.
    b. ☐ I'm interested in learning more, but as yet I have not committed my life to Jesus.
    c. ☐ Other ....

3. **If you have not yet become a Christian, what is stopping you?**
    ....
    ....

4. **Have you reached the place in your spiritual life where you know for certain that you have eternal life? If
    you died tonight, would you go to heaven?**

    ☐ YES   ☐ NO

5. **Suppose you were to die tonight and you stood before God in heaven and he asked, 'Why should I let
    you into heaven?' What would you reply?**

    'You should let me in because ....
    ....
    ....
    ....

6. **Quite often, people who have finished this course want to go on and discover more about the Christian
    faith. To cater for this need, we offer a further six-week course, which looks at what it means to be a
    disciple, a follower of Jesus Christ. Would you be interested in doing this course?**

    ☐ YES   ☐ NO   ☐ YES, BUT LATER

7. a. ☐ I am satisfied with the church I go to.
    b. ☐ I do not regularly attend church, but I would like to be introduced to a church where there is warm
        fellowship and good teaching.
    c. ☐ I do not wish to attend church at this stage.

8. **What comments would you like to make about the course, either positive or negative?**
    ....
    ....
    ....
    ....
    ....
    ....

MARK'S GOSPEL
The twenty most asked questions

1. What are demons, or evil spirits? Mark 1:23–27

The Bible takes seriously the reality of an unseen spiritual world. This spiritual world has both a good side and an evil or malignant side.

The Devil, or Satan, is not just some impersonal evil force at work in world. The Bible depicts Satan as personal and powerful. His work is totally opposed to God and directed against God's people.

Evil spirits and demons mentioned in the gospels are the Devil's agents in this work. Although Satan and his angels are immensely powerful, the New Testament shows Jesus to be Lord over Satan, and to have defeated him through his death and resurrection.

2. Why did Jesus tell healed people not to tell anyone? Mark 1:34; 7:36

Jesus did not want to become like a side-show with people coming just to see signs and wonders. He rejected such people (Mark 8:11–13, John 4:48). If people would not respond to the preaching of the kingdom of God calling for repentance and faith (Mark 1:15), miracles alone would not convince them.

Miracles attract people, and it is possible that Jesus saw that the curious crowds would hamper his ministry, which is just what happened (Mark 1:45).

3. Why did Jesus call himself the Son of Man? Mark 2:10

Jesus wanted to identify with mankind, so he preferred to be called Son of Man rather than being called Son of God. Son of Man is a Jewish term meaning simply 'a man'. The prophet Ezekiel was often called 'son of man' in this sense (Ezek. 33:1).

Son of Man is also a well-known title used in the Old Testament for the Messiah (Daniel 7:13–14). In this vision Daniel saw 'one like a son of man' (i.e. like a human being). God then gives to this son of man an eternal kingdom over all the nations of the earth.

The religious leaders in Jesus' day would have interpreted Jesus' use of Son of Man as a veiled claim to be the coming Messiah, the fulfilment of Daniel's prophecy.

4. New cloth, old coat; new wine, old skins. Mark 2:21–22

People were complaining that Jesus was not observing the religious rules and traditions of his day (Mark 2:18). The Pharisees had literally thousands of laws and religious regulations, and they taught that a person had to observe these rigorously in order to please God.

Jesus was saying that the faith he had come to bring was totally incompatible with the Pharisees' system. Jesus could not be 'fitted into' their legalistic religion. He came to bring a living relationship with God, not rules; grace, love and peace, not religious formulas.

Christianity is not a religion. 'Religion' is from the Latin word meaning 'rules.' Christianity is not a set of rules, but a personal relationship with the Living God.

5. What is the 'eternal sin'? Mark 3:29

The context here is the key. The religious leaders had observed Jesus' miracles and heard his teaching at first hand. However, their assessment of Jesus was: 'He has Beelzebub' (Mark 3:22) — an old name for the Devil.

They had hardened their hearts against the work of God's Spirit through the ministry of Jesus. This unrepentant, continuous attitude is the 'blasphemy against the Holy Spirit' (Mark 3:29 R.S.V.).

This has nothing to do with swearing at the Holy Spirit — in simple terms it means continuously to reject Jesus' claim in a person's heart and life.

For this there can be no forgiveness, for they have refused the only way of forgiveness that God has provided.

Of course, it is only unforgivable for as long as a person goes on doing it. Many of the religious leaders did repent later on, and so were forgiven (Acts 6:7).

This is a vital personal concept. If I reject Jesus, I can never be forgiven!

6. Why did Jesus teach in parables? Mark 4:10–12

Many people have trouble with this passage. On the surface it sounds as if Jesus taught in parables so that people would not understand, which would be very strange indeed.

However, we need to see that there are two groups mentioned here: the disciples and 'those outside'. The disciples were spiritually intrigued by the parables and drawn nearer to Jesus to hear the explanation. There is a spiritual principle here — 'to those who have will more be given'.

However, to 'those outside' the band of disciples, the parables just remained baffling stories. Their spiritual interest was not aroused. They 'hear, but do not understand'.

All people are either like moths or bats. They are either attracted to the light of Jesus' teaching, or repelled by it. Jesus' words, including his parables, always act in this two-fold way. See also Mark 4:33–34.

7. Did Jesus have brothers and sisters? Mark 6:3

This passage mentions four brothers by name and at least two sisters. These were presumably the natural children of Joseph and Mary conceived after the birth of Jesus. See also Mark 3:32.

Some Christians hold that Mary remained a virgin after the birth of Jesus, and that the brothers and sisters mentioned here are really cousins. The Greek word *adelphoi* can also mean 'cousins'. However, Matt 1:25 seems to imply that Joseph and Mary had a normal sexual relationship after Jesus' birth.

8. Throwing the children's food to the dogs? Mark 7:24–30

The key to this difficult passage lies in the fact that the woman was not a Jewess — she was a Gentile, from near the pagan city of Tyre (verses 24, 26).

Jesus' ministry at this stage was exclusively to the Jews, the chosen descendants of Abraham. He forbade his disciples, at this period, to preach to the Gentiles or Samaritans (Matt.10:5).

Jesus says to her: 'Let us first feed the children. It isn't right to take the children's food and throw it to the dogs.'

The term 'children' here refers to the Jews and 'dogs' was a common, unflattering expression for any Gentile person. So Jesus is saying in fact: 'It isn't right to take what belongs to the Jews and give it to you Gentiles.'

In her reply in verse 28 the woman is, in effect, saying: 'Yes Lord — I acknowledge that as a Gentile woman I have not claim upon you, the Jewish Messiah. But at least give me a few moments of your time to deal with a problem I have!'

Jesus is impressed by her faith and her persistence and grants her request (Matt.15:28).

The term 'dogs' seems hard from the lips of Jesus. One writer says: 'The Lord's use of the conventional Jewish term dogs for Gentiles does not mean that he recognised this description as accurate. He desired to see whether the woman was ready to take such a lowly position in order to win healing.'

9. What is the yeast of the Pharisees and the yeast of Herod? Mark 8:15

'Yeast' means influence. Just as a tiny amount of yeast has a big effect on the whole batch of dough, so Jesus warns against the 'yeast' of the Pharisees and Herod.

The Pharisees were the most influential religious party in Jesus' day, though they were few in number. They taught that rigorous law-keeping was the path to God. Jesus called them 'hypocrites', which means 'play-actors', for their public displays of religion and self-righteousness.

On the yeast of Herod one writer says: 'The yeast of Herod is adultery, murder, hastiness in swearing, affectation in piety and hatred of Christ and his forerunner (John the Baptist).'

So, Jesus is warning against outward religious show (the Pharisees), and crass worldliness (Herod).

10. 'And you still don't understand?' Mark 8:17–21

Twice Jesus had fed large crowds of Jewish people in a desert place where no food was available. Surely, as Jews, they would have been reminded of the way God fed the children of Israel under the leadership of Moses, and gave them the manna in the desert.

Surely, too, they would have remembered Moses' prophecy towards the end of his life: 'The Lord your God will raise up for you a prophet like me from among you' (Deut. 18:15). Could the disciples not yet understand that Jesus was the predicted Moses-like prophet, in fact the prophesied Messiah?

It is perhaps no accident that in the very next section Peter declared: 'You are the Messiah' (Mark 8:29). The penny has dropped, at last!

11. What is 'The kingdom of God come with power'? Mark 9:1

This is probably a reference to the coming of the Holy Spirit on the day of Pentecost. After his resurrection Jesus said to his disciples: 'When the Holy Spirit comes upon you, you will be filled with power' (Acts 1:8).

The kingdom of God came with the entry of Jesus into the world. It came with power at the pouring out of God the Holy Spirit.

12. Who is Elijah? Mark 9:11-13

In the last statement of the Old Testament, God promised that he would send again Elijah the prophet before the day of the Lord! (Mal. 4:5–6). Elijah was a prophet in the 8th century B.C., and he dressed in a distinctive way, wearing animal skins and a leather girdle (2 Kings 1:8).

When John the Baptist appeared he was dressed in a similar manner (Matt. 3:4). Jesus makes it clear that John was the fulfilment of the prophecy concerning Elijah.

Does this mean that John was a prophet like Elijah, or that John was Elijah actually come back to life again? Probably the former, though it is not made clear in the gospels.

13. What does it mean to cut off your hand, etc.? Mark 9:43–48

Jesus obviously did not intend that a Christian should physically cut off a hand or foot, or pluck out an eye!

In this dramatic way, Jesus says: If anything is stopping you from entering the kingdom of God, it is better to take drastic and perhaps sacrificial action to rid yourself of that impediment, whatever it is, than to end up in hell for ever.

The logic is obvious: temporary pain is better than eternal punishment!

14. Divorce — what does Jesus say? Mark 10:1–12

Jesus is making it clear that divorce is always against the perfect purpose of God. God's plan, since creation, is that married people should live together for the whole of their lives (verses 6–9). This is God's perfect plan.

Jesus also emphasised that if people institute divorce because they have found a nicer partner, such action is adultery (verses 11–12).

However, because people's hearts are still hard (verse 5) divorce has always taken place. The danger is that we can start to treat divorce as the unforgivable sin, where a divorced person can never again be acceptable to God.

Christ came to die for all sin, including the sin of divorce. In talking to the Samaritan woman in John chapter 4, Jesus knew that she had already been divorced five times and was now living with a sixth man. No doubt in some of these divorces the woman had been in the wrong. But even knowing these facts, Jesus still freely offered her acceptance and forgiveness: 'If you knew the gift of God, and who it is that is saying to you, "Give me a drink", you would have asked him and he would have given you living water' (John 4:10).

It is not our role to be moral policemen. Like Jesus, we must freely hold out the water of forgiveness, cleansing and eternal life.

If the subject of divorce becomes a major issue in your *Christianity Explained* group, it may be advisable to arrange an extra session, and involve a minister or counsellor who can explain the biblical position lovingly.

15. Why did Jesus curse the fig tree? Mark 11:12–14; 20–25

This action has perplexed many Christians, as it was Jesus' only destructive miracle. Two suggestions can be made:

(a) Jesus was teaching his disciples about the power of prayer. Certainly that was the interpretation that he himself gave in the following verses (verses 22–24). Jesus was saying in effect: 'This power is available to you too. If you say to this hill...etc.'

(b) Many commentators have suggested that we have here what is called an acted parable or a parable without words! Many such acted parables were used by the Old Testament prophets. In verse 11 Jesus went to the Temple, which should have been the most spiritual place on earth. He looked around on everything and saw in fact spiritual bankruptcy — a commercial racket going on.

The next day he cleansed the Temple (verses 15–19). Wedged between these two incidents is the cursing of the fig tree.

Some suggest that the fig tree is Israel and the Temple worship. Instead of finding spiritual fruitfulness in the Temple, he found barrenness, like the fig tree. Just as the fig tree was cursed, so too Israel would come under God's curse and condemnation for her spiritual emptiness.

This idea of the coming destruction of the Temple is taken up more fully in chapter 13.

The Temple and the city of Jerusalem were destroyed by the Roman armies in A.D. 70, about 37 years later.

16. One bride for seven brothers? Mark 12:18–27

What is the point of this trick question? In Jesus' day there were two major religious parties: the Pharisees, who believed in life after death; and the Sadducees, who said that death was the end — there was no hope of life beyond the grave, or resurrection (verse 18).

The Sadducees thus came up with this question (verses 18–23). In his answer to them in verses 24–27 Jesus says two things: *first*, there is life beyond the grave, but no marriage relationship as such. This does not mean that married couples will not know each other in heaven — just that sexual relationships will have ended. *Second*, God did not say: 'I was the God of Abraham, Isaac, Jacob...' but, 'I am the God of Abraham...' I am still their God, because they live on! The hope of the resurrection is the central Christian hope.

17. What is the 'awful horror'? Mark 13:14

Fortunately, this is one case where the parallel passage in another gospel, in this case Luke, gives us the key. Luke chapter 21 is the parallel passage to Mark chapter 13. Luke has a tendency in his gospel to explain difficult words or expressions.

In the place of Mark 13:14, Luke has these words: 'When you see Jerusalem surrounded by her armies...then those who are in Judea must run away to the hills.'

So in the place of 'awful horror', Luke has 'Jerusalem surrounded by her armies'.

In A.D. 65 the Roman armies surrounded Jerusalem after a political uprising. After a terrible five-year war, the Roman armies entered the city, desecrated the Holy of Holies in the Temple, then proceeded to pull down both the Temple and the city. Jesus' words in Mark chapter 13 came to pass.

18. Why did Jesus not know the date of his own return? Mark 13:32

Some people have suggested that, because Jesus did not know the date of his own return, this means that he is less than perfect, less than divine. Since God is omniscient (knows everything), Jesus cannot therefore be God.

Two comments need to be made: *first*, there is a great mystery here. When 'the word became flesh', Jesus 'emptied himself' (Phil.2:7). As a baby and child, Jesus had to grow in wisdom, just like all human children do. He was not born with a complete knowledge built in. It is probably fair to say that Jesus would have known nothing about computers or internal combustion engines. *Second*, it is not sinful to lack knowledge. It is sinful to make dogmatic statements on the basis of little or no real knowledge. Jesus freely acknowledged that he did not know the date of his return.

If he did not know, we should never speculate!

This is one of those little touches which verifies the truth of the Bible. If someone was making up the story of Jesus Christ, he would never have left in Mark 13:32.

19. Was the darkness an eclipse? Mark 15:33

It has been suggested that the darkness over the cross of Jesus was caused by a daytime eclipse of the sun.

However, this idea is not possible. Jesus was crucified at the time of the Jewish Passover, which is always at full moon. At full moon, the heavenly bodies are in an almost straight line like this: sun - Earth - Moon.

To have a daytime eclipse of the sun the bodies must be in an exact straight line like this: Sun — Moon — Earth.

Physically we cannot explain this account of darkness adequately. Sufficient to say that it was in keeping with mankind's darkest deed!

20. Why are there odd endings to Mark's Gospel? Mark chapter 16

Most scholars agree that Mark's Gospel ends abruptly at verse 8 in a rather unsatisfactory manner. The women have seen the empty tomb and been informed of the resurrection of Jesus, but there is no account of Jesus himself appearing, as there is in the other three gospels.

The long endings of Mark's Gospel appear to be attempts by well-meaning scribes to add some resurrection appearances to Mark. However, even the style of the Greek original changes after verse 8.

This does not mean that what is contained in verses 9 to the end is wrong or fictional, and many of the details here can be double-checked from the other gospels. It just means that they were probably not in Mark's original.

Copying masters for handout sheets...

The sheets on the next six pages are summaries of each study. Permission is given for groups to photocopy these sheets. They are designed to be folded as shown:

The reading plans may be copied on to the back, if appropriate. At the conclusion of each study, one sheet should be given to each member of the group.

Session 1.

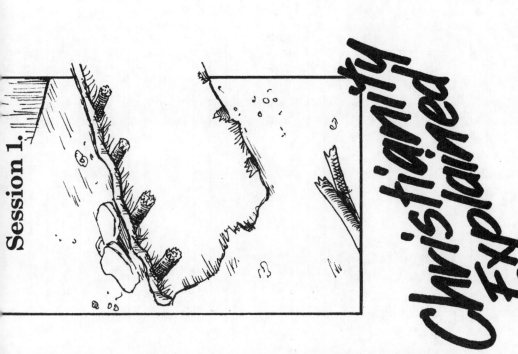

Jesus – Son of God

'This is the Good News about Jesus Christ, the Son of God'.

Mark 1.1

This is God's world, and we have seen that Jesus comes into the world with all the authority of God himself. We have seen:

1. Jesus' authority as a teacher
Mark 1:21-22

2. Jesus' authority over evil spirits
Mark 1:23-28

3. Jesus' authority over sickness
Mark 1:29-31

4. Jesus' authority to forgive sins
(This shows him to be equal with God)
Mark 2:1-12

5. Jesus' authority over nature
Mark 4:35-41

6. Jesus' authority over life and death
Mark 5:35-42

But most importantly, as far as we are concerned today, we have seen:

7. Jesus' authority over people
Mark 1:16-20

Conclusion:

We have seen in this study:

• Jesus' great authority as the Son of God.

• Jesus' claim to be divine, that is, God.

• The call for us to follow him.

Someone has called Jesus 'The man you can't ignore'. He is either a *liar*, a *lunatic* or the *Lord*.

There are three concepts which you must believe to be a Christian. We have seen the first of these:

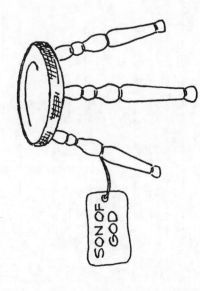

At home:

Read Mark chapters 1 to 5. Note anything you do not understand, or would like to discuss. There will be a time for discussing these things at the beginning of next week's session.

Mark Chapters 1-5

Suggested Reading Plan

Try to jot down what you think are the main points the passage is making. Also list any things you have questions about (??) and any things that strike you as being interesting (!!). We will discuss them at the start of the next session.

1. Mark 1: 1 – 28
Main Points _____

??

!!

2. Mark 1: 29 – 2:12
Main Points _____

??

!!

3. Mark 2: 13 – 3: 6
Main Points _____

??

!!

4. Mark 3: 7 – 34
Main Points _____

??

!!

5. Mark 4: 1 – 41
Main Points _____

??

!!

6. Mark 5: 1 – 20
Main Points _____

??

!!

7. Mark 5: 21 – 43
Main Points _____

??

!!

Any thoughts on Mark Chapters 1 – 5 as a whole

!!

Jesus—his death on the cross

1. The facts of the cross
Read Mark 15:21-39.

2. The meaning of the cross

a) The darkness (15:33)
Indicates that, in the death of Jesus, God was doing a special, supernatural act.

b) The cry (15:34-37)
'Why did you abandon me?' We see that at least to some extent, God had forsaken or abandoned his Son when he was on the cross.

Remember the book, which we imagined was a record of every time we have lived our way instead of God's way. Jesus, who always lived his Father's way, 'bore our sins in his body on the cross', and our sins formed a barrier between him and his Father. Jesus dealt with our sins and their guilt and punishment, and his resurrection showed that God was satisfied with the sin-bearing that Jesus had completed on the cross.

c) The curtain (15:38)
The tearing of the curtain indicated that people come back into relationship with God only through Jesus' death.

d) The ransom (10:45)
This is the price Jesus paid to buy us back to God—that price was the giving of his life, that is, his death.

Conclusion:

Jesus' death is sufficent for the sins of anyone, but God's forgiveness is not automatically given to everybody. Each of us must individually accept by faith the Jesus of the cross.

There are three basic concepts which you must believe to be a Christian. We have now seen two of these:

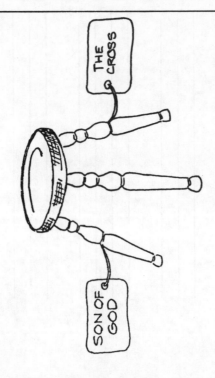

At home:

Read Mark chapters 6 to 10. Note anything you do not understand, or would like to discuss. There will be a time for discussing these things at the beginning of next week's session.

Mark Chapters 6–10

Suggested Reading Plan

Try to jot down what you think are the main points the passage is making. Also list any things you have questions about (??) and any things that strike you as being interesting (!!). We will discuss them next week.

1. Mark 6: 1-29
Main Points _____

??

!!

2. Mark 6: 30-56
Main Points _____

??

!!

3. Mark 7: 1-37
Main Points _____

??

!!

4. Mark 8: 1-38
Main Points _____

??

!!

5. Mark 9: 1-32
Main Points _____

??

!!

6. Mark 9: 33-10:16
Main Points _____

??

!!

7. Mark 10: 17-52
Main Points _____

??

!!

Any thoughts on Mark Chapters 6 - 10 as a whole

Session 3.

Christianity Explained

Jesus – his resurrection

---

1. The resurrection predicted

Read Mark 10:32-34.

2. The facts of the resurrection

In the Bible there are recorded at least ten occasions when the risen Jesus appeared to his followers. He spoke to them, ate with them, was touched by them (e.g. Luke 24:36-43).

3. The meaning of the resurrection

Read Acts 10:39-43.

a) *All people will be raised*
'the living and the dead'

b) *All people will be judged*
'judge of the living and the dead'

c) *The risen Jesus will be the judge*
'he is the one God has appointed judge'

d) *All will be divided into two groups*
'everyone who believes...sins forgiven'

'If a person is ashamed of me...I will be ashamed of him'

(Mark 8:38)

Conclusion:

Jesus' attitude to me on the day of judgment is the same as my attitude to him now, in this life.

If I *accept* him *now*, he will *accept* me *then*.

If I *reject* him *now*, he will *reject* me *then*.

There are three basic concepts which you must believe to be a Christian. These are:

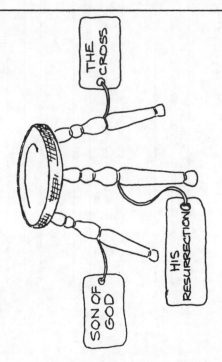

At home:

Read Mark chapters 11 to 16. Note anything you do not understand, or would like to discuss. There will be a time for discussing these things at the beginning of next week's session.

Mark Chapters 11 - 16

Suggested Reading Plan

Try to jot down what you think are the main points the passage is making. Also list any things you have questions about (??) and any things that strike you as being interesting (!!). We will discuss them during the next session.

1. Mark 11: 1-33
Main Points _____

??

!!

2. Mark 12: 1 - 44
Main Points _____

??

!!

3. Mark 13: 1 - 37
Main Points _____

??

!!

4. Mark 14: 1 - 52
Main Points _____

??

!!

5. Mark 14: 53 - 15:15
Main Points _____

??

!!

6. Mark 15: 16 - 47
Main Points _____

??

!!

7. Mark 16
Main Points _____

??

!!

Any thoughts on Mark Chapters 11 - 16 as a whole

Session 4.

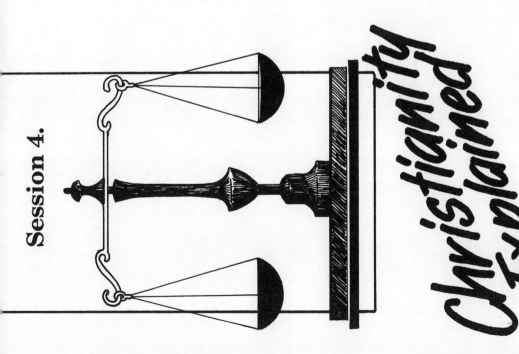

Christianity Explained

God's gift – not our works

Imagine that you have just died, and that God is judging your life. God says to you: 'Give me one good reason why I should accept you into heaven with me?' What would you reply?

The wrong answer: What I have done

God, you should accept me because I have:

- Lived a good life
- Kept the Ten Commandments
- Given to charities
- Been a good citizen
- Been a good parent
- Prayed and read the Bible
- Been to church
- Been baptised...etc.

Mark 7:20-23

3. The right answer: What Christ has done

God, you should accept me because of what Christ has done for me, and that alone.

Good works do not produce salvation

BUT

Salvation produces good works.

Read Ephesians 2:8-10.

Conclusion:

We have seen that eternal life, forgiveness of sins and a place in God's kingdom cannot be earned or deserved by us. They have been earned for people by the Son of God, through his death and rising again.

NOT

| WHAT I HAVE DONE |

BUT

| WHAT CHRIST HAS DONE |

So forgiveness and eternal life is the free gift of God to all who will receive the giver—that is, Jesus Christ.

Next week we will discuss how we do this. This is the vital question, WHAT IS A CHRISTIAN?

At home:

Read the booklet you have been given. Note anything you do not understand and would like to discuss. Also re-read these passages from Mark's Gospel and underline what you think are the most significant words for you:

a) Mark 1:15
b) Mark 8:34-38
c) Mark 9:43-48
d) Mark 10:29-31

Session 5.

Christianity Explained

What is a Christian?

1. Repenting

Repentance means:

I PUT JESUS FIRST...

...BEFORE MY WILL

...BEFORE MY AMBITIONS

...BEFORE MY POPULARITY

...BEFORE ANYONE·ANYTHING ELSE

See Mark 8:34-38 and Mark 9:43-48

At home:

Re-read the booklet you have been given.

What gifts does God promise to those who repent and believe?

Mark 1:8 H___ S_____

Mark 2:10 F_____

Mark 10:30 E_____ L___

'The kingdom of God is at hand, repent and believe the good news.' Mark 1:15

REVIEW

Q: What is a Christian?

A: Someone who belongs to the kingdom of God.

Q. How can I belong to the kingdom of God?

A: Repent and believe in Jesus Christ.

We have seen that a Christian believes certain facts about Jesus Christ:

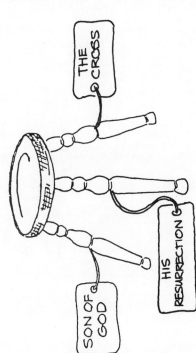

THE CROSS

SON OF GOD

HIS RESURRECTION

But being a Christian is more than just believing these facts.